VEGETABLE DELIGHTS

by

Johna Blinn

Edited by Tom Dorsey

**Published by Playmore Inc., Publishers and Waldman Publishing Corp.,
New York, New York**

PRINTED IN CANADA

Edited by Joshua Hanft

Cover Photo: John Paul Endress/Int'l Stock Photo

Acknowledgments

The author is indebted to the following for assistance in making this a useful cookbook: Olive Dempsey, A.C. Collins, Bess Roberts, Anita Mizner, Caryl Saunders, Claire Boasi, Ruth Lundgren, Anita Fial, Judy Bean, Marjorie Z. Ashby, Chris Pines, Yvonne Martin, Lillian Newcomb, Lois Westlund, Pat Mason, Gretchen Ziesmer, United Fresh Fruits and Vegetables Association, Fresh Garlic Association, Stokely-Van Camp, Inc., Planter's Peanut Oil, Karo Corn Syrup, Fresh Tomato Marketing Board, American Spice Trade Association, American Mushroom Institute, California Artichoke Advisory Board, Mirro Corporation, Lea & Perrins, Campbell Soup Co., Angostura International Limited, Standard Brands, Tuna Research Foundation, Lawry's Foods, Inc., Idaho Potato Commission, Chun King Foods and New Zealand Lamb Company, Inc.

J.B.

BARONET
B·O·O·K·S

BARONET BOOKS is a trademark of Playmore Inc., Publishers and Waldman Publishing Corp., New York, N.Y.

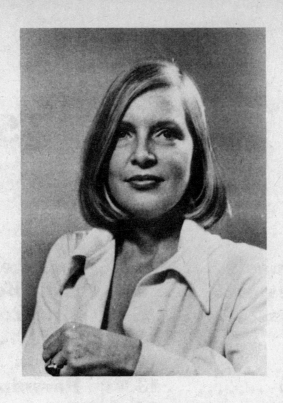

The Author

To many of the top movie and television stars, Johna Blinn is a celebrity. For almost 20 years they have welcomed her into their homes, onto sets, just about anywhere to talk about food, entertaining and lifestyles. Her column, "Celebrity Cookbook," is syndicated throughout the world and appears weekly in more than 140 newspapers and periodicals. A collection of hundreds of these conversations and recipes appears in *Celebrity Cookbook*, published by Waldman Publishing Corporation. Currently, Johna Blinn is writing a series on Celebrity Food-styles for *FAMILY CIRCLE*, America's largest supermarket magazine (circulation, 20 million), where she has already profiled Tom Brokaw, Angela Lansbury, John Madden, Michael Landon, Robert Urich, Raymond Burr, Steve Garvey, Diane Sawyer and others.

Blinn is a former assistant food editor of LOOK magazine and is the author of a number of books, including *The Shangri-la Cookbook, Fabulous Appetizers, Fabulous Soups, Fabulous Salads, Fabulous Vegetarian Recipes, Fabulous Poultry & Game, Fabulous Meats, Fabulous Fish & Seafood, Fabulous Desserts, Fabulous Low Calorie Recipes, Fabulous Oriental Recipes, Fabulous Oven & Stovetop Recipes,* and *Fabulous Italian Recipes,* all published by Waldman Publishing Corporation. In addition, Blinn is a frequent contributor of up close and personal interviews, profiles and entertainment features to *USA TODAY* and other American and foreign newspapers and magazines.

A graduate of the State University of Iowa, Blinn took graduate work in Home Economics at the University of Wisconsin and taught home economics in Iowa, Virginia and New York. Now based in Los Angeles, she is married to a nationally known newspaper syndicate editor, writer and management consultant, and they have two grown children.

CONTENTS

Acorn Squash 5
Artichokes 5
Asparagus 6
Beans 8
Beets 11
Bok Choy 13
Broccoli 14
Brussels Sprouts ... 15
Cabbage 16
Carrots 18
Cauliflower 20
Celery 23
Chicory 24
Collard Greens 24
Corn 25
Dandelions 27
Eggplant 27
Escarole & more ... 27
Jicama 28
Kale 29
Kohlrabi 29
Leeks 30
Lentels 30

Lettuce 31
Lima Beans 31
Mushrooms 33
Okra 35
Onion 35
Parsnip 37
Peas 37
Potatoes 38
Pumpkin 42
Radish 42
Rutabaga 42
Soybeans 43
Spinach 43
Squash 46
Sweet Potatoes 48
Tomatoes 51
Turnips 53
Vegetable Medley .. 53
Watercress 59
Yams 59
Zucchini 60
Vegetable Butters
   & Sauces 62

Glazed Acorn Squash

Serves 2

2 medium acorn squash, halved and seeded	1 tablespoon margarine, melted
1½ cups water	½ teaspoon ground cinnamon
⅓ cup light corn syrup	dash of salt

1. Place squash, cut-side down, in a 13 × 9 × 2-inch baking dish; add water.
2. Bake in a preheated 400° F. oven 30 minutes, or until squash is firm.
3. Drain water; turn cut-side up.
4. Stir together corn syrup, margarine, cinnamon and salt in a small bowl; spoon corn syrup mixture evenly over squash.
5. Bake in preheated 350° F. oven, basting occasionally, 15 minutes, or until fork-tender.

Artichokes Aurora with Vinaigrette Sauce

Serves 2

2 tablespoons olive oil	½ teaspoon thyme
½ pound spinach, washed and trimmed	¼ teaspoon salt
¼ pound mushrooms, sliced	pinch of pepper
¼ cup chopped onion	⅓ cup slivered almonds
1 small clove garlic, minced	2 small artichokes
¼ cup grated Parmesan cheese	1 lemon or lime, sliced
	Vinaigrette Sauce (page 12)

1. Heat oil in a skillet; sauté spinach several minutes.
2. Add mushrooms, onion and garlic; continue to cook 5 minutes over high heat, stirring often, until no liquid appears in bottom of skillet.
3. Remove from heat.
4. Add Parmesan cheese, thyme, salt and pepper; mix well.
5. Stir in almonds; set aside.
6. Prepare artichokes:
   a. Cut off stems even with base; break off small leaves at base and discard.
   b. Cut 1 inch off top, straight across; with scissors, snip off tip of each leaf.
   c. Holding artichoke upright, run under cold water, spreading leaves apart.
   d. Rub all cut surfaces with lemon to prevent discoloration.
   e. With fingers, carefully open center leaves; turn artichokes over on a board; press down firmly at base to spread leaves open.
   f. Turn artichokes right side up; pull out yellow leaves from center.
   g. With a spoon, scrape out prickly portion from heart; set aside.
7. Place a thin slice of lemon in bottom of cavity of each artichoke; fill cavities with spinach filling.
8. Place artichokes in a deep baking dish; pour 2 cups water around them.
9. Cover and bake in preheated 375° F. oven 45 minutes.
10. Serve hot with Vinaigrette Sauce.

Vinaigrette Sauce

Makes ¾ cup dressing

½ cup olive oil
¼ cup freshly squeezed lemon
   or lime juice (juice of
   1 lemon or lime)

1 small clove garlic, minced
¼ teaspoon dried leaf thyme
¼ teaspoon salt
¼ teaspoon ground pepper

1. Combine oil, lemon or lime juice, garlic, thyme, salt and pepper in a covered container; cover and shake.
2. Let stand 30 minutes before using.

Asparagus 'n Tomatoes Stir-Fry

Serves 6

1 tablespoon peanut oil
1 pound asparagus, diagonally
   sliced into 1½-inch pieces
4 green onions, diagonally
   sliced into 1-inch cubes
1½ cups sliced fresh
   mushrooms

1 tablespoon water
1 teaspoon cornstarch
1 tablespoon teriyaki
   barbecue marinade
½ teaspoon seasoned salt
2 firm tomatoes, cut into
   thin wedges

1. Heat oil in a wok or large skillet.
2. Add asparagus; stir-fry until almost tender, about 5 minutes.
3. Add green onions and mushrooms; stir-fry 2 minutes longer.
4. Blend together in a small bowl, water, cornstarch, marinade and salt.
5. Push vegetables to sides of wok or skillet; add cornstarch mixture to center and heat until bubbly.
6. Stir vegetables into cornstarch mixture; continue stirring until thickened.
7. Add tomatoes; heat through.

Asparagus Vinaigrette

Serves 4

1 tablespoon sugar
1 teaspoon salt
1 teaspoon paprika
1 teaspoon dry mustard
¼ teaspoon pepper
¼ cup cider vinegar
¾ cup corn oil
dash of onion powder

1 tablespoon sweet pickle
   relish
1 tablespoon chopped
   pimientos
1 can (14½ ounces) cut
   asparagus spears, drained
hard-cooked eggs (optional
   garnish)

1. Combine sugar, salt, paprika, mustard, pepper, vinegar, oil, onion powder, pickle relish, and pimientos in a jar with a tight lid; shake to mix well.
2. Pour dressing over well-drained asparagus; let marinate in refrigerator several hours before serving.
3. Garnish with chopped hard-cooked eggs if desired.

Asparagus with Sauce Nouvelle

Serves 4

1 pound fresh asparagus　　　　　**½ teaspoon salt**

Sauce Nouvelle

1. Break off each stalk of asparagus as far down as it snaps easily; remove scales with a knife.
2. Wash thoroughly, using a brush.
3. Tie stalks of asparagus in a bundle with a string; stand upright in bottom part of a double boiler.
4. Sprinkle with salt; add 1½ inches boiling water.
5. Cover with top part of double boiler, inverted; steam 15 to 20 minutes, or until just crisp-tender.
6. Lift out by catching string with tines of a fork; drain and cut strings.
7. Arrange asparagus on a serving platter; serve hot with Sauce Nouvelle.

Sauce Nouvelle

Makes 1 cup sauce

1 tablespoon vegetable oil　　　　**¼ cup heavy cream**
1 small onion, sliced　　　　　　　**¼ cup chopped fresh parsley**
1 clove garlic, minced　　　　　　　**¼ teaspoon dried leaf basil**
2 tomatoes, peeled, seeded　　　　　**¼ teaspoon salt**
**　and chopped**　　　　　　　　　　　**⅛ teaspoon pepper**

1. Heat oil in a small skillet; sauté onion and garlic until tender.
2. Add tomatoes, heavy cream, parsley, basil, salt and pepper; bring to a boil.
3. Simmer, uncovered, 5 minutes until sauce thickens slightly, stirring occasionally.
4. Serve over fresh asparagus.

Fresh Asparagus Custard

Serves 4

1 pound fresh asparagus　　　　　　**2 tablespoons melted butter**
boiling water　　　　　　　　　　　**　or margarine**
2 eggs　　　　　　　　　　　　　　**1 teaspoon salt**
1 cup milk　　　　　　　　　　　　**⅛ teaspoon freshly ground**
1 tablespoon minced fresh onion　　**　pepper**

1. Break off asparagus stalks as far down as they snap easily; wash asparagus.
2. Cook asparagus, covered, in a small amount of boiling water until just tender; drain if necessary.
3. Cool; chop finely.
4. Beat eggs; stir in milk, onion, butter, salt, pepper and asparagus.
5. Turn into 4 buttered baking cups (6-ounce capacity); set cups in pan of hot water.
6. Bake in preheated 300° F. oven 50 to 60 minutes, or until silver knife inserted in center comes out clean.
7. Run sharp knife around sides to unmold.

7

Snappy Green Beans

Serves 8

1 can (10¾ ounces) condensed
    cream of mushroom soup
⅓ cup milk
1½ teaspoons original
    Worcestershire sauce
1 teaspoon onion powder

2 packages (9 ounces each)
    frozen French-style green
    beans, cooked and drained
⅓ cup coarsely crumbled
    corn chips

1. Combine soup, milk, Worcestershire sauce and onion powder in a saucepan; cook over low heat, stirring constantly, 5 minutes.
2. Pour over hot green beans; sprinkle with corn chips.

Swiss Beans

Serves 6

2 tablespoons butter or
    margarine
1 tablespoon all-purpose
    flour
¼ teaspoon salt
dash of pepper
½ teaspoon instant minced
    onion

½ cup dairy sour cream
1 can (16 ounces) sliced
    French-style green beans,
    drained
1 cup grated process Swiss
    cheese (about ¼ pound)
1 cup crushed cornflakes

1. Melt 1 tablespoon butter in a saucepan; add flour, salt, pepper, onion and sour cream.
2. Gently stir in green beans; place in a 1-quart casserole.
3. Cover with cheese.
4. Melt remaining tablespoon of butter; mix with cornflakes.
5. Sprinkle cornflakes over grated cheese.
6. Bake, uncovered, in preheated 350° F. oven 20 minutes.

Three-Bean Bake

Serves 8

½ cup chopped onion
1 tablespoon butter or
    margarine
1 can (16 ounces) pork and
    beans
1 can (16 ounces) lima beans,
    drained

1 can (15 ounces) dark red
    kidney beans
½ cup tomato catsup
2 tablespoons brown sugar
1½ teaspoons vinegar
1 teaspoon dry mustard
1 teaspoon salt

3 strips bacon, diced

1. Sauté onion in butter until tender.
2. Stir sautéed onion together with remaining ingredients except bacon in a 13 × 9 × 2-inch pan.
3. Top with bacon; bake, uncovered, in preheated 350° F. oven 1¼ hours.

Savory Green Beans-Corn Casserole

Serves 6

1 package (10 ounces) frozen
   French-cut green beans,
   thawed
1 package (10 ounces) whole
   kernel corn, thawed
2 cups shredded American
   cheese
½ cup minced celery
½ cup chopped green pepper

½ cup mayonnaise
2 tablespoons minced onion
½ teaspoon salt
½ teaspoon marjoram
½ teaspoon dill weed
⅛ teaspoon white pepper
1 tablespoon butter or
   margarine, melted
½ cup bread crumbs

1. Combine green beans, corn, cheese, celery, green pepper, mayonnaise, onion, salt, marjoram, dill weed and pepper in a bowl; blend well.
2. Turn vegetables into a buttered 2-quart casserole.
3. Mix butter with crumbs; sprinkle over vegetables.
4. Bake, covered, in preheated 350° F. oven 30 minutes.
5. Uncover; continue baking 15 to 20 minutes longer, or until crumbs are golden brown and mixture is bubbly.

Sauced Wax Beans

Serves 8

1 can (10¾ ounces)
   Cheddar cheese soup,
   condensed and
   undiluted
2 cans (15½ ounces each)
   cut wax beans, drained
1 can (16 ounces) small whole
   white onions, drained

1 jar (2 ounces) sliced
   pimientos, drained
½ cup seasoned bread crumbs
1 tablespoon butter or
   margarine (for garnish)

1. Heat cheese soup in a 2-quart saucepan until warmed through.
2. Add beans, onions and pimientos to soup; heat to serving temperature.
3. Sauté bread crumbs in butter in a small skillet until lightly browned.
4. Place cheese-vegetable mixture in a serving dish; garnish with bread crumbs.

Snap Beans with Nutmeg Butter

Serves 6

1½ pounds fresh snap beans
1 inch boiling water
1 teaspoon salt

3 tablespoons butter or
   margarine
¼ teaspoon ground nutmeg
⅛ teaspoon ground black pepper

1. Wash snap beans; cut off tips and cut into 1-inch pieces.
2. Place beans in a saucepan with boiling water and salt; bring to a boil and boil 5 minutes.
3. Cover and continue cooking until just crisp-tender, about 10 minutes.
4. Drain; toss lightly with butter, nutmeg and ground black pepper.

Clustered Bean & Corn Salad

Serves 8

1 can (1 pound 4 ounces) red
kidney beans, drained
1 can (1 pound) whole kernel
corn, drained
1 package (9 ounces) frozen cut
green beans, cooked and
drained
½ cup oil

2 tablespoons original
Worcestershire sauce
2 tablespoons wine vinegar
1 teaspoon prepared brown
mustard
¾ teaspoon salt
½ teaspoon sugar
½ teaspoon curry powder

crisp lettuce (optional)

1. Arrange kidney beans, corn and green beans in a large serving bowl; set aside.
2. Combine remaining ingredients in a small container; mix well.
3. Pour mixture over vegetables; cover and refrigerate 2 hours, or longer.
4. Serve on lettuce-lined salad plates if desired.

Fresh Pole Beans with Sesame Seeds

Serves 8

1 pound fresh pole beans
water
½ teaspoon salt

2 tablespoons butter or
margarine
1 teaspoon sesame seeds

¹⁄₁₆ teaspoon ground black pepper

1. Wash and remove tips from pole beans; leave whole.
2. Place beans in a saucepan with ½-inch depth boiling water and salt; bring to a boil.
3. Cook, uncovered, 5 minutes.
4. Cover and cook 5 minutes longer, or until crisp-tender.
5. Drain, if necessary.
6. Melt butter in a saucepan; add sesame seeds and black pepper.
7. Cook, tossing lightly, until sesame seeds are golden brown.
8. Serve over hot beans.

Refried Beans

Serves 4 to 5

1 can (1 pound 4 ounces)
refried beans
1 package (1¼ ounces) taco
seasoning mix
¼ cup water

¾ cup grated mild Cheddar
cheese (for garnish)
¼ cup finely chopped onion
(for garnish)

1. Combine refried beans, taco seasoning mix and water in a saucepan; bring to a boil.
2. Reduce heat and simmer 5 minutes.
3. Garnish bean mixture with grated cheese and chopped onion just before serving.

Shanghai Bean Sprout Salad

Serves 4 to 6

2 medium tomatoes, cut in
  wedges
1 cucumber, skin scored and
  thinly sliced
1 avocado, pared and sliced
3 cups fresh bean sprouts
crisp salad greens (for
  garnish)
½ cup corn oil

2 tablespoons fresh lemon
  juice
2 tablespoons vinegar
¾ teaspoon salt
¼ teaspoon sugar
½ teaspoon dry mustard
dash of pepper
3 strips cooked bacon,
  crumbled (optional)

1. Combine tomato wedges, cucumber slices, avocado slices and bean sprouts in a salad bowl; garnish edges of bowl with salad greens.
2. Just before serving, mix oil, lemon juice, vinegar, salt, sugar, dry mustard and pepper; pour over salad.
3. Sprinkle with crumbled bacon if desired.

Beet-Root Pancakes

Makes 12 pancakes

1 cup minced cooked fresh
  beets
2 tablespoons cornstarch
4 egg yolks, beaten
3 tablespoons heavy cream or
  undiluted evaporated milk

½ teaspoon sugar
1 teaspoon salt
½ teaspoon ground nutmeg
fruit marmalade or
  preserves

1. Combine all ingredients in a mixing bowl; mix well.
2. Bake, in pancake fashion, on a hot buttered griddle or in heavy skillet.
3. Serve with fruit marmalade or preserves.

Caraway Seed Fresh Beets

Serves 4

2 cups cooked sliced fresh
  beets
2 tablespoons butter or
  margarine
1 tablespoon fresh lemon
  juice

½ teaspoon salt
1/16 teaspoon ground black
  pepper
½ teaspoon whole caraway seed
¼ cup dairy sour cream
  (optional)

1. Place all ingredients except sour cream in a saucepan; heat only until warm.
2. Serve at once with dollops of sour cream if desired.

11

Cranberry Beets

Serves 6

1 can (16 ounces) diced
    beets, drained
1 can (16 ounces) whole berry
    or jellied cranberry sauce

2 tablespoons orange juice
1 teaspoon grated orange
    rind
dash of salt

1. Combine all ingredients in a saucepan; heat thoroughly, stirring occasionally.
2. Serve at once.

NOTE: Delicious with turkey or ham!

Dutch-Style Beets

Serves 6

2 teaspoons minced onion
2 tablespoons butter
1 tablespoon flour
salt to taste
pepper to taste

1 tablespoon sugar
1 cup beet liquid
2 tablespoons vinegar or
    lemon juice
2½ cups diced beets, drained

1. Sauté onion in butter 5 minutes; add flour and blend.
2. Add seasonings, sugar, beet liquid and vinegar; cook until thick, stirring constantly.
3. Add beets; heat thoroughly.

Harvard Beets

Serves 6

3 tablespoons cornstarch
⅓ cup sugar
¾ teaspoon salt
1½ cups beet liquid (or beet
    liquid plus water)

2 tablespoons vinegar
1½ tablespoons butter or
    margarine
3 cups sliced cooked or
    canned beets

1. Mix cornstarch, sugar and salt.
2. Blend in beet liquid, vinegar and butter; cook over moderate heat, stirring constantly, until thickened.
3. Add beets to sauce; let stand 10 minutes, if desired, to blend flavors.
4. Heat to serving temperature.

Honeyed Beets

Serves 4

2 tablespoons butter or
    margarine, melted
1 teaspoon cornstarch
3 tablespoons honey
2 tablespoons water

1 teaspoon lemon juice
dash of salt
1 can (16 ounces) tiny whole
    beets, drained

1. Melt butter in a saucepan; blend in cornstarch.
2. Stir in honey, water, lemon juice and salt; cook over medium heat, stirring constantly, until mixture thickens and comes to a boil.
3. Add beets, turning to coat; cover and cook just until heated through.

Chinatown Sweet & Sour Bok Choy

Serves 4 to 6

3 tablespoons corn oil
1 head bok choy, washed, trimmed and cut in 1-inch pieces
¼ cup light brown sugar

¼ cup red wine vinegar
1 teaspoon minced fresh ginger root
1 tablespoon cornstarch
1 tablespoon soy sauce

½ cup water

1. Heat oil in a large skillet or wok; add bok choy and stir-fry over high heat 1 minute.
2. Combine brown sugar, vinegar and ginger; add to skillet.
3. Mix well; cover and steam 1 minute.
4. Combine cornstarch and soy sauce with water; add to skillet.
5. Cook and stir until thickened.

Broccoli Sauté

2 pounds fresh broccoli
½ cup water
¼ cup peanut oil

2 cloves garlic, minced
1 teaspoon salt
⅛ teaspoon pepper

1. Wash broccoli.
2. Split ends of large stalks lengthwise into halves or quarters, depending on size.
3. Place broccoli in a large skillet; sprinkle with water, peanut oil, garlic, salt and pepper.
4. Cover tightly; cook over very low heat 20 to 25 minutes, or until stalks are tender, turning broccoli several times during cooking.

Broccoli Spears with Mustard Sauce

Serves 3 to 4

1 package (10 ounces) frozen broccoli spears
⅓ cup mayonnaise

2 teaspoons prepared yellow mustard
1 teaspoon sugar

1. Cook broccoli according to package directions; drain and chill.
2. Combine remaining ingredients; mix thoroughly.
3. Serve sauce over chilled broccoli.

NOTE: Sauce can also be served over cooked cauliflower. For a tasty hot dish, serve vegetables piping hot and top with sauce at room temperature.

Broccoli with Piquant Sauce

Serves 6 to 8

2 pounds broccoli
boiling salted water
2 tablespoons minced onion
2 tablespoons minced pimiento
4 tablespoons butter

¼ teaspoon salt
⅛ teaspoon pepper
2 tablespoons fresh lemon
juice

1. Trim broccoli by removing any large outer leaves and cutting off the stalks. If stalks are large in diameter, gash twice at right angles from the base towards heads, taking care not to cut apart.
2. Cook broccoli, uncovered, in boiling salted water 10 minutes, or until tender.
3. Sauté onion and pimiento in butter in a skillet; add salt, pepper and lemon juice.
4. Drain broccoli; pour hot sauce over it.
5. Serve at once.

Broccoli alla Romano

Serves 4 to 6

¼ cup olive oil
1 teaspoon minced garlic
6 cups (2 pounds) fresh broccoli flowerets, with stems

1½ cups dry white wine
½ teaspoon salt
freshly ground black pepper

1. Heat oil in a large heavy skillet until a light haze forms.
2. Remove pan from heat; stir garlic in hot oil 30 seconds.
3. Return to moderate heat; toss broccoli in oil until flowerets glisten.
4. Add wine, salt and pepper; simmer, uncovered, stirring occasionally, 5 minutes.
5. Cover skillet and simmer 15 minutes until broccoli is tender.
6. Transfer flowerets with slotted spoon to a bowl or deep platter.
7. Boil liquid left in skillet over high heat until reduced to ½ cup; pour over broccoli.

NOTE: Delicious served with dry white wine!

Broccoli Stir-Fry

Serves 4

1 bunch fresh broccoli
2 tablespoons vegetable oil
2 tablespoons soy sauce
1 teaspoon cornstarch
1 tablespoon honey

½ teaspoon freshly grated
ginger root or ¼ teaspoon
ground ginger
¼ teaspoon Tabasco sauce
¼ cup slivered almonds

1. Wash broccoli; cut off broccoli flowerets.
2. Peel broccoli stems; slice stems ¼-inch thick.
3. Heat oil in a large skillet or wok; stir-fry broccoli 5 minutes until crisp-tender.
4. Combine soy sauce and cornstarch in a small bowl; add honey, ginger and Tabasco sauce.
5. Pour mixture over broccoli; cook until sauce thickens slightly.
6. Stir in almonds.

Brussels Sprouts with Peanut Sauce

Serves 4

1 pound fresh brussels
 sprouts
½ cup boiling salted water

¼ cup butter or margarine
2 tablespoons chopped
 unsalted peanuts

1. Cook brussels sprouts, covered, in a small amount of boiling salted water until just tender; drain if necessary.
2. Meanwhile, melt butter; stir in chopped peanuts.
3. Pour over brussels sprouts.

Brussels Sprouts Royal

Serves 4

1 package (10 ounces) frozen
 brussels sprouts
2 tablespoons butter or
 margarine

¼ cup fine dry bread crumbs
1 hard-cooked egg yolk, sieved
2 teaspoons snipped parsley

1. Cook sprouts according to package directions; drain.
2. Meanwhile, melt butter in a small saucepan until it begins to brown; add crumbs, egg yolk and parsley.
3. Spoon mixture over hot sprouts; toss lightly and serve.

Brussels Sprouts Lancaster

Serves 8

1 quart brussels sprouts
1 cup white seedless
 grapes, stemmed and washed

butter
salt
paprika

1. Inspect sprouts carefully, removing tough outer leaves.
2. Cook sprouts, uncovered, in boiling water until just tender. (To test, pierce with a toothpick.)
3. Add grapes; drain thoroughly.
4. Season with butter, salt and paprika.
5. Serve at once.

Devilish Brussels Sprouts

Serves 4

1 package (10 ounces) frozen
 brussels sprouts
1 tablespoon prepared mustard
1 teaspoon soy sauce

2 teaspoons original
 Worcestershire sauce
½ teaspoon salt
dash of pepper

1. Cook brussels sprouts according to package directions.
2. Meanwhile, combine remaining ingredients in a medium-size saucepan; simmer 2 to 3 minutes.
3. Drain sprouts; place in serving dish.
4. Spoon sauce over sprouts and serve.

Sprouts Amandine

Serves 4

1 package (10 ounces) frozen
brussels sprouts
3 tablespoons butter or
margarine

¼ cup slivered almonds
½ teaspoon tarragon
1 tablespoon lemon juice

1. Prepare brussels sprouts according to package directions; drain and keep warm.
2. Melt butter in a medium-size skillet; sauté almonds until lightly browned.
3. Add tarragon; stir.
4. Sprinkle lemon juice over brussels sprouts; add sprouts to skillet, tossing lightly.
5. Sauté briefly to reheat; transfer to serving dish.

Wine-Braised Cabbage & Potatoes

Serves 4

½ small head cabbage,
cut into 4 wedges
8 small new potatoes,
cut in half
½ cup dry white wine

2 tablespoons butter or
margarine
1 tablespoon fresh minced
parsley
¼ teaspoon salt

1. Combine all ingredients in a large skillet; bring to a boil.
2. Reduce heat and simmer, covered, 15 minutes, or until potatoes are tender.

Hungarian Cabbage

Serves 6

2 slices bacon
1 pound cabbage, coarsely
shredded (2 quarts)

¾ teaspoon salt
pepper (optional)
2 tablespoons vinegar

2 tablespoons water

1. Fry bacon until crisp; remove from pan and set aside.
2. Add remaining ingredients to fat in pan; cover tightly and cook slowly, stirring occasionally, 20 to 25 minutes. Cabbage should be tender-crisp.
3. Crumble bacon over top before serving.

Cabbage Creole

Serves 4

½ medium-size head cabbage,
cut into bite-size pieces
1 can (16 ounces) stewed
tomatoes, cut up

¼ cup water
salt to taste
⅛ teaspoon pepper

1. Combine all ingredients in a skillet; cook on medium-high until cabbage is desired tenderness, about 15 minutes.
2. Serve at once.

German Sweet & Sour Red Cabbage

Serves 8

4 tablespoons butter
8 cups shredded red cabbage
¼ cup sherry
1 teaspoon salt
⅛ teaspoon pepper
1 cup minced onion

2 tablespoons sugar
⅓ cup peeled and grated
   tart apples
¼ cup white raisins, soaked
   45 minutes in cold water,
   then drained

1 cup currant jelly

1. Melt butter in a skillet over medium heat.
2. Add remaining ingredients except jelly; stir well.
3. Cover, reduce heat and simmer 40 minutes.
4. Add jelly; cover and simmer 20 minutes longer.

Hot Cabbage Slaw

Serves 6

⅓ cup water
2 beef bouillon cubes
1 medium-size (about
   ½ pound) green cabbage,
   coarsely shredded

½ cup chopped onion
½ cup grated carrot
2 tablespoons wine vinegar
2 teaspoons original
   Worcestershire sauce

½ teaspoon caraway seed

1. Combine water and bouillon cubes in a large saucepan; bring to boil, stirring to dissolve bouillon cubes.
2. Add cabbage; reduce heat and simmer, covered, 10 minutes.
3. Add remaining ingredients; simmer, covered, until cabbage is tender, about 10 minutes longer.

Red Cabbage with Apples

Serves 8 to 10

¼ cup margarine
½ cup chopped onion
3 pounds red cabbage,
   shredded (3 quarts)
⅓ cup light corn syrup

2 tablespoons cider vinegar
1 tablespoon salt
1 cup Burgundy wine
2 tart apples, peeled, cored
   and sliced

1 cup red currant jelly

1. Melt margarine in a 5-quart Dutch oven over medium-high heat; add onion and cook 3 minutes, stirring frequently, or until tender.
2. Add cabbage, corn syrup, vinegar and salt; cook, stirring occasionally, 15 minutes.
3. Stir in wine; bring to a boil.
4. Reduce heat and simmer 30 minutes, or until cabbage is tender.
5. Add apples and jelly; stir until jelly is melted.
6. Simmer 15 minutes longer.

Carrots Caribbean

Serves 3 to 4

2 cups fresh carrots, cut in thin strips
¾ cup pineapple juice
¾ teaspoon ground cinnamon
1/16 teaspoon ground black pepper
1/8 teaspoon ground nutmeg

1. Combine carrots, pineapple juice, black pepper, nutmeg and cinnamon in a medium-size saucepan; bring to a boil.
2. Reduce heat and simmer, covered, until carrots are crisp-tender, about 15 minutes.

Candied Carrots

Serves 6

1½ pounds fresh carrots or 1 package (1½ pounds) frozen cut or small whole carrots
boiling salted water
1/8 teaspoon ground mace
1 tablespoon butter or margarine
½ cup orange marmalade
1 tablespoon lemon juice

1. If fresh:
   a. Scrape carrots and remove ends.
   b. Cut into 2 × 3/8-inch strips or crosswise into ¼-inch slices.
   c. Cook in a small amount of boiling salted water, covered, until tender, 12 to 15 minutes for strips, 8 to 10 minutes for slices.
2. If frozen, cook according to package directions; drain thoroughly.
3. Melt butter in a large skillet; stir in orange marmalade, lemon juice and mace.
4. Add carrots; cook over low heat, turning several times, until evenly glazed and heated.

Carrot Cookies with Orange Icing

Makes 2 to 3 dozen cookies

¾ cup butter or margarine
¾ cup sugar
1 egg, beaten
1 cup cold mashed cooked carrots
2 cups sifted all-purpose flour
2 teaspoons baking powder
¼ teaspoon salt
1 teaspoon pure vanilla extract
1/3 cup chopped walnuts
Orange Icing

1. Cream together butter and sugar until fluffy.
2. Add egg and carrots; blend well.
3. Stir in dry ingredients.
4. Stir in vanilla and nuts; mix well.
5. Drop by teaspoons on ungreased cookie sheet; bake in preheated 400° F. oven 20 minutes.
6. Cool on wire racks before frosting with Orange Icing.

Orange Icing

3 tablespoons melted
butter

juice and grated rind of
1 orange

1 cup confectioner's sugar

1. Combine butter, orange juice and rind.
2. Add sugar, beating until icing is desired thickness.

Carrot Casserole I

Serves 8

2½ pounds carrots, sliced
boiling water
2½ cups Cheddar cheese cubes

1 large onion, sliced
½ cup margarine, melted
bread crumbs

1. Blanch carrots in boiling water; remove and drain.
2. Layer carrots, cheese and onion in a buttered casserole dish; drizzle margarine over each layer.
3. Sprinkle with bread crumbs.
4. Freeze.
5. Before baking, thaw in refrigerator.
6. Bake, uncovered, in preheated 325° F. oven 40 minutes.

Carrot Casserole II

Serves 8

2 cans (16 ounces each) sliced
carrots, well drained
1 can (10¾ ounces) condensed
cream of celery soup,
undiluted

1 cup grated American cheese
½ cup dry bread crumbs
2 tablespoons butter or
margarine, melted

1. Combine carrots, soup and cheese in a 1½-quart casserole.
2. Mix bread crumbs and melted butter together; sprinkle over top of casserole.
3. Bake in preheated 350° F. oven 25 to 30 minutes.

Orange-Glazed Carrots & Celery

Serves 6 to 8

½ cup light or dark corn
syrup
⅓ cup margarine
1 teaspoon grated orange rind
¼ cup orange juice

2 pounds carrots, cut in 2-inch
pieces, cooked
6 ribs celery, cut in 1-inch
pieces

1. Heat corn syrup, margarine, orange rind and juice in a large skillet over medium heat until margarine is melted; stirring occasionally, cook 10 minutes, or until thickened.
2. Add carrots and celery; stirring occasionally, cook 8 to 10 minutes, or until glazed.

Carrots, Sweet & Sour

Serves 6

1½ pounds whole baby carrots,
  peeled and trimmed
water
⅓ cup honey
⅓ cup fresh lemon juice
1 cup slivered red or green
  bell pepper

⅛ teaspoon cardamom
⅛ teaspoon cloves
⅛ teaspoon cinnamon
⅛ teaspoon ginger
⅛ teaspoon seasoned salt
⅛ teaspoon lemon pepper
1½ tablespoons Marsala wine

1. Parboil carrots in water until almost tender; drain.
2. Combine remaining ingredients to make a glazed sauce.
3. Cook carrots in sauce until tender and glazed, stirring occasionally.

Cauliflower Polonaise

Serves 6

1 large cauliflower
1 teaspoon lemon juice or
  vinegar
boiling water
¾ cup fine bread crumbs

6 tablespoons butter
1 tablespoon minced parsley
¼ teaspoon salt
¼ teaspoon paprika
dash of ground white pepper

¾ cup grated cheese

1. Trim leaves, stalks and core from cauliflower.
2. Place cauliflower in a saucepan filled with lemon juice and boiling water to nearly cover head; cover and cook until cauliflower is barely cooked.
3. Drain; keep hot.
4. Meanwhile, sauté bread crumbs in butter until golden.
5. Add parsley, salt, paprika and white pepper.
6. Put cauliflower in a serving bowl; spoon crumb mixture evenly over cauliflower.
7. Dust with grated cheese; serve at once.

Cauliflower with Tomatoes

Serves 4 to 6

1 large cauliflower, broken
  into flowerets
1 small clove garlic, chopped
3 tablespoons olive oil

½ teaspoon salt
½ cup chopped tomatoes
1 teaspoon chopped parsley
2 tablespoons Parmesan cheese

1. Boil cauliflower until tender; drain.
2. Sauté garlic in olive oil until browned; remove garlic.
3. Add flowerets to olive oil; sauté lightly.
4. Add salt and tomatoes; cover and simmer 5 minutes.
5. Arrange in a serving dish; sprinkle with parsley and cheese.

Cauliflower, Spanish Main

Serves 6

1 medium-size head fresh
   cauliflower or 2 packages
   frozen cauliflower
water
salt
3 tablespoons butter or
   margarine
3 tablespoons flour

2 teaspoons Angostura aromatic
   bitters
1½ cups milk
1 package (3 ounces) soft
   cream cheese
parsley sprigs (optional
   garnish)

1. Remove outer leaves and stalks of fresh cauliflower; break into flowerets.
2. Soak cauliflowerets in cold water 15 minutes; drain.
3. Place in saucepan and cover with cold water; add ½ teaspoon salt per cup of water, bring to a boil, and cook 10 minutes. Drain.
4. If frozen, cook cauliflower according to package directions.
5. Meanwhile, prepare cream sauce:
   a. Melt butter in a saucepan over very low heat; add flour and ¾ teaspoon salt, stirring until smooth.
   b. Mix Angostura bitters with milk; gradually add to flour mixture, stirring constantly to avoid lumps.
   c. Cook, stirring, until smooth and thickened.
6. Add cooked cauliflower to sauce; pour mixture into a buttered baking dish.
7. Dot top with pieces of cream cheese; bake in preheated 400° F. oven until sauce bubbles and cheese is slightly browned.
8. Garnish with parsley if desired.

Cheesey Cauliflower & Peas

Serves 6

1 package (10 ounces) frozen
   cauliflower
1 package (9 ounces) frozen
   green peas
1 tablespoon butter or
   margarine
1 tablespoon all-purpose
   flour

½ cup milk
½ cup grated American cheese
1½ teaspoons original
   Worcestershire sauce
cayenne to taste
1 jar (2 ounces) sliced
   pimientos, drained (for
   garnish)

1. Cook cauliflower and peas according to package directions; drain and set aside.
2. Melt butter in a medium-size saucepan; add flour and stir briskly.
3. Add milk; heat, stirring constantly, until thickened and bubbly.
4. Remove from heat; stir in cheese, Worcestershire sauce and cayenne, stirring constantly until cheese is melted.
5. Return pan to low heat; add reserved vegetables and cook 2 minutes.
6. Spoon into serving bowl; garnish with pimientos.

21

Fresh Cauliflower-Chestnut Casserole

Serves 6

1 medium-size head cauliflower
(1½ pounds)
1 inch boiling water
1¼ teaspoons salt
1 pound chestnuts* or ¾ cup
sliced blanched almonds

2 tablespoons butter or
margarine
¼ teaspoon ground white
pepper
2 tablespoons hot water

1. Break cauliflower into flowerets; place in a saucepan with 1 inch boiling water and 1 teaspoon salt.
2. Bring to a boil, uncovered; cook 5 minutes.
3. Cover and cook until about ¾ done; drain.
4. Put a layer of cauliflower in a buttered casserole; cover with a layer of chestnuts and dot with butter.
5. Sprinkle lightly with white pepper mixed with ¼ teaspoon salt.
6. Continue layering until all ingredients are used.
7. Add 2 tablespoons hot water.
8. Bake, covered, in preheated 350° F. oven 30 minutes.

*To prepare chestnuts: Prick with a fork or split top end in a cross slit. Place them in a preheated 350° F. oven or in a slightly greased skillet. Cover and cook over low heat until outer shell cracks. Shell, while warm, and cook in boiling salted water until tender. (The brown coating around chestnuts will come off during the boiling process.) Chop medium-fine.

Hurry-Curry Cauliflower

Serves 4

1 medium-size head cauli-
flower (1½ pounds)

½ cup water
¼ teaspoon salt

Hurry-Curry Sauce

1. Wash cauliflower; remove green leaves and cut slice off stem end.
2. Combine water and salt in a 1½-quart covered microwave-proof casserole; place cauliflower in casserole, stem-side down.
3. Microwave on HIGH 12 to 15 minutes, turning cauliflower halfway through cooking time.
4. Remove to a serving platter; let stand 5 minutes before serving.
5. Serve with Hurry-Curry Sauce.

Hurry-Curry Sauce

Makes 1 cup sauce

3 egg yolks
2 tablespoons light cream or
milk
1 to 2 tablespoons freshly
squeezed lemon juice

½ teaspoon curry powder
¼ teaspoon salt
½ cup butter or margarine,
melted

1. Combine egg yolks, cream, lemon juice, curry powder and salt in an electric blender; process 10 seconds until smooth.
2. With blender on slow speed, gradually add melted butter; process 10 seconds longer until sauce is smooth and slightly thickened.
3. Serve immediately.

NOTE: Conventional cooking method: Prepare cauliflower as above. In a large saucepan, cook, covered, in 1 inch boiling, salted water 20 to 30 minutes until tender.

Creamed Celery & Onions

Serves 6

1 bunch celery with leaves	**½ teaspoon salt**
1 bay leaf	**⅛ teaspoon white pepper**
2 sprigs parsley	**3 tablespoons corn oil**
1 pound pearl onions, peeled	**½ cup milk**
3 cups water	**3 tablespoons cornstarch**
2 chicken-flavored bouillon cubes	**¼ cup slivered almonds**

1. Cut 4 inches from the top of celery bunch; rinse.
2. Tie celery tops, bay leaf and parsley together with string; set aside.
3. Trim base from remaining celery bunch; scrub stalks.
4. Diagonally slice celery stalks ½-inch thick.
5. Put celery tops, onions, water, bouillon cubes, salt and pepper in a 2-quart saucepan; bring to a boil.
6. Cover and simmer 20 minutes, or until onions are tender.
7. Discard celery tops.
8. Heat oil in a large skillet over medium heat; add celery and cook 2 minutes.
9. Add onions and broth.
10. Stir milk into cornstarch until smooth; add to skillet.
11. Stirring constantly, bring to boil over medium heat; boil 1 minute.
12. Sprinkle with almonds and serve.

Fruited Celery

Serves 6

1 stalk celery	**1 apple, diced**
3 tablespoons butter or margarine	**½ cup golden raisins**
⅓ cup chopped onion	**1 tablespoon original Worcestershire sauce**
1¼ teaspoons salt	

1. Separate celery into ribs; cut off leaves (save for soups and stews).
2. Slice ribs diagonally into 1-inch pieces (makes about 6 cups).
3. Melt butter in a large skillet; add onion and celery.
4. Sauté until tender, about 5 minutes.
5. Mix in apple, raisins, Worcestershire sauce and salt; stir-fry until celery is crisp-tender, about 5 minutes.

Celery-Bean Casserole

Serves 6

1 cup sliced celery
¼ cup chopped onion
1 can (16 ounces) pork and
  beans
¼ teaspoon celery seed
1 tablespoon brown sugar

1 tablespoon original
  Worcestershire sauce
1 tablespoon prepared mustard
3 dashes of Tabasco sauce
¾ cup French-fried onion rings
1 clove garlic, crushed

1. Cover the bottom of a 1½-quart casserole dish with celery and onion.
2. Combine remaining ingredients except onion rings; pour over celery layer.
3. Bake, covered, in preheated 350° F. oven 30 minutes.
4. Remove cover; top with onion rings and bake, uncovered, about 5 minutes, or until onions are browned.

Italian-Style Chicory

Serves 4 to 6

1 head chicory
3 tablespoons olive oil
¼ cup chopped fresh onion
1 clove garlic, crushed

¼ teaspoon dried leaf
  oregano
¼ cup packaged seasoned
  bread crumbs

2 tablespoons grated Parmesan cheese

1. Wash chicory; drain.
2. Heat oil in a large saucepan; add onion, garlic and oregano.
3. Cut chicory into 1-inch pieces; add to heated oil.
4. Cover and simmer over low heat 15 minutes, stirring occasionally. As chicory cooks, it will produce a small amount of liquid. This may be drained off, if desired.
5. Mix together bread crumbs and Parmesan cheese; sprinkle over cooked chicory and mix lightly.

Fresh Collard Greens with Bacon

Serves 6

2 pounds fresh collard
  greens
½ cup boiling water
½ teaspoon salt

3 tablespoons bacon fat
3 strips crisp bacon,
  crumbled

1. Cut off coarse stems of collards; wash and cut into 2- to 3-inch lengths.
2. Place in a saucepan with water, salt and bacon fat; cover and cook only until tender, 30 minutes. (Cooking time depends upon age of the greens.)
3. Remove from heat and toss lightly with crumbled crisp bacon.
4. Serve hot.

Corn Pudding

Serves 6

½ cup sugar
1 full teaspoon cornstarch
¼ cup butter or margarine,
   melted
2 eggs, beaten

1 cup milk
¾ teaspoon salt
1 can (16 ounces) creamed
   corn
1 teaspoon pure vanilla extract

1. Mix sugar and cornstarch; add melted butter.
2. Add beaten eggs, milk and salt.
3. Stir in corn and vanilla.
4. Bake in preheated 375° F. oven until brown on top, about 30 to 35 minutes.

Fresh Corn & Oyster Casserole

Serves 4 to 6

3 cups (4 ears) fresh corn,
   cut off the cob
½ cup soft bread crumbs
1 cup drained oysters (fresh
   or frozen)
1 egg, beaten

1¼ teaspoons salt
1 teaspoon whole celery seed
⅛ teaspoon ground black
   pepper
4 tablespoons butter or
   margarine

1. Combine corn, ¼ cup bread crumbs, oysters, egg, salt, celery seed and pepper.
2. Break 2 tablespoons butter into small pieces; add to corn mixture.
3. Turn mixture into a greased 1-quart casserole.
4. Melt remaining butter; mix with remaining crumbs.
5. Sprinkle crumbs over top of casserole.
6. Bake in preheated 350° F. oven 40 minutes, or until crumbs are brown and corn is tender.

Foiled Corn, Grilled

Serves 4 to 6

6 ears young, tender sweet
   corn
butter or margarine,
   softened

salt to taste
pepper to taste
water

1. Strip off corn husks and remove silk.
2. Brush ears evenly with softened butter; season liberally with salt and pepper.
3. Place each ear on a double thickness of foil; sprinkle with a few drops of water.
4. Wrap foil securely around corn, sealing tightly.
5. Place corn on grill; cook over medium coals 15 to 20 minutes, turning often to cook evenly. (Can also be oven-roasted in preheated 350° F. oven about same length of time.)

NOTE: Delicious eating!

Corn 'n Pepper Fritters

Makes about 24 fritters

1 egg
½ cup milk
1 can (12 ounces) golden whole
　kernel corn with sweet
　peppers, undrained
peanut oil

1½ cups unsifted all-purpose
　flour
1 tablespoon baking powder
1 teaspoon salt
dash of pepper
syrup (optional)

1. Beat egg in a large bowl; stir in milk, corn and 1 tablespoon peanut oil.
2. Add and beat in flour, baking powder, salt and pepper.
3. Drop by tablespoonfuls into deep or shallow hot peanut oil heated to 375° F.; fry until golden brown, 2 to 3 minutes on each side.
4. Drain on paper towels; serve hot. (If desired, serve with syrup.)

Cool Corn Salad

Serves 4 to 6

¼ cup dairy sour cream
¼ cup mayonnaise
1 tablespoon prepared mustard
2 teaspoons white vinegar
1 teaspoon sugar
¼ teaspoon salt
⅛ teaspoon pepper
1 can (17 ounces) golden whole
　kernel corn, drained
1 jar (2 ounces) sliced
　pimientos, drained and diced
2 carrots, peeled and grated
½ cup diced onion

1. Make dressing by combining sour cream, mayonnaise, mustard, vinegar, sugar, salt and pepper in a medium-size bowl.
2. Add remaining ingredients; toss to blend.
3. Cover and refrigerate 1 hour.

Corn O' Plenty in Toast Cups

Serves 4 to 5

2 tablespoons butter or
　margarine
1 jar or package (about
　3 ounces) dried beef,
　shredded
2 tablespoons minced onion
1 tablespoon all-purpose flour
¾ cup milk
1 can (17 ounces) cream-style
　golden corn
½ cup shredded sharp Cheddar
　cheese
2 tablespoons minced green
　pepper
Toast Cups (page 37) or toast

1. Melt butter in a skillet; sauté beef and onion until beef begins to curl.
2. Remove from heat; blend in flour.
3. Stir in milk; cook over medium heat until thickened.
4. Add corn; heat through.
5. Stir in cheese and green pepper; heat until cheese melts.
6. Serve in Toast Cups or over toast.

Kale Colcannon

Serves 6

2 pounds potatoes (6 medium)
boiling water
1 bunch fresh kale
1 egg
2 tablespoons grated fresh
onion

¼ cup milk
2 tablespoons butter or
margarine
1 teaspoon salt
⅛ teaspoon pepper

1. Cook potatoes in boiling water to cover 30 to 40 minutes, or until very tender; drain, cool and peel.
2. Place potatoes in a large bowl; mash well.
3. While potatoes are cooking, wash kale and remove coarse stems.
4. Put kale in a large saucepan with 1 cup boiling water; cover and cook 5 minutes.
5. Drain and chop kale.
6. Add chopped kale to potatoes in bowl; add egg and remaining ingredients, beating until smooth.
7. Reheat in a large saucepan over low heat, stirring almost constantly.

Herbed Fresh Kale

Serves 6

2 pounds fresh kale
2 tablespoons minced onion
¾ teaspoon salt
½ teaspoon ground marjoram

½ teaspoon sugar
⅛ teaspoon ground black
pepper
2 tablespoons bacon fat

1. Wash kale; cut off all tough stems.
2. Place kale in a saucepan with onions, salt, marjoram, sugar and black pepper; cover and cook 20 minutes, or until tender.
3. Add bacon fat; mix well and serve.

Jan's Creamed Kohlrabi

Serves 6

8 small kohlrabi
½ cup boiling water
½ teaspoon salt

2 tablespoons butter or
margarine
¼ cup heavy cream

white pepper to taste

1. Carefully wash kohlrabi; remove tops with a sharp knife and remove any discolored leaves or tough stems.
2. Chop greens; peel and dice bulbs.
3. Drop diced kohlrabi into boiling salted water in a saucepan; cover and simmer 5 to 7 minutes, or until nearly tender.
4. Add greens; cook, uncovered, until greens are barely cooked.
5. Drain, reserving cooking liquid for soup.
6. Add butter and cream; heat until butter is melted.
7. Season to taste with more salt and white pepper.
8. Serve at once.

29

Baked Leeks in Cheese Sauce

Serves 6

2 pounds leeks
salted water
¼ cup plus 3 tablespoons
grated Cheddar cheese

3 cups Medium White Sauce
freshly ground black pepper
salt
buttered bread crumbs

1. Wash and slice leeks; soak in salted water.
2. Meanwhile, stir ¼ cup grated cheese into Medium White Sauce; heat and stir until cheese is melted and sauce is smooth.
3. Spoon sauce into buttered 1-quart casserole.
4. Put leeks in sauce; cover with remaining cheese.
5. Sprinkle cheese liberally with pepper and salt; top with buttered crumbs.
6. Bake, uncovered, in preheated 350° F. oven 30 minutes, or until brown on top.

Medium White Sauce

Makes about 1 cup

2 tablespoons flour
2 tablespoons butter or
margarine, melted

1 cup milk
salt to taste
pepper to taste

1. Blend flour into butter in a saucepan or skillet; cook and stir until a smooth paste.
2. Gradually add milk, stirring constantly; cook until thickened.
3. Season to taste with salt and pepper.

Honey-Baked Lentils

Serves 6 to 8

1 pound uncooked lentils
water
1 teaspoon dry mustard
¼ teaspoon ginger
2 tablespoons soy sauce

½ teaspoon freshly ground
black pepper
1 yellow onion, chopped
6 slices lean bacon
½ cup honey

1. Add lentils to a saucepan with 2½ quarts water; bring to boil and cook 30 minutes.
2. Drain lentils, reserving some of the cooking liquid.
3. Put lentils in a greased 2-quart casserole.
4. Combine mustard, ginger, soy sauce and pepper in a small bowl; pour over lentils.
5. Scatter chopped onions over lentils.
6. Cut bacon into julienne strips; toss over top of lentils and onions.
7. Pour honey over all.
8. Cover tightly and bake in preheated 350° F. oven 1 hour 55 minutes.
9. Remove lid and bake 5 to 10 minutes longer. (During cooking add reserved liquid if lentils seem too dry.)

Lettuce & Radish Slaw

Serves 8

½ cup dairy sour cream
½ cup mayonnaise
1 tablespoon prepared
  yellow mustard
2 tablespoons chopped
  fresh onion
1 tablespoon fresh lemon
  juice

½ teaspoon salt
⅛ teaspoon Tabasco pepper
  sauce
1 tablespoon dill weed
8 cups shredded iceberg
  lettuce (1 large head)
2 cups sliced radishes

1. Combine sour cream, mayonnaise, mustard, onion, lemon juice, salt, Tabasco and dill weed in small jar; cover and shake to mix well.
2. Chill.
3. To serve, combine lettuce and radishes in a large bowl; add dressing, tossing to mix well.

Lettuce Medley Parisienne

Serves 4

1 pound white onions
¼ cup boiling water
1½ pounds fresh green peas,
  shelled

¼ cup butter or margarine
1 head lettuce
1 teaspoon salt
⅛ teaspoon pepper

1. Peel onions and place in a saucepan with boiling water; cover and cook 3 minutes.
2. Add peas and butter; cover and cook 3 minutes.
3. Cut lettuce into 4 wedges; place over peas.
4. Sprinkle with salt and pepper, cover and cook 5 minutes.
5. Serve immediately.

Savory Lima Beans

Serves 6

2 slices bacon
1 tablespoon flour
½ teaspoon sugar
1 can (16 ounces) stewed
  tomatoes

1 can (16 ounces) fordhook
  green lima beans,
  drained
salt to taste

1. Cook bacon until crisp; drain on paper towel, reserving 2 tablespoons drippings in skillet.
2. Mix flour and sugar; add to skillet, stirring to blend.
3. Add tomatoes and lima beans; heat, stirring constantly, until mixture thickens slightly and is heated through.
4. Add salt to taste.
5. Place in serving dish; top with crumbled bacon.

Lima Bean Creole with Variations

Serves 6

2 packages (10 ounces each)
  frozen lima beans
6 slices bacon
¼ cup minced onion

2 tablespoons chopped green
  pepper
½ teaspoon salt
pepper as desired

2 cups cooked or canned tomatoes

1. Cook beans as directed on package; drain.
2. Fry bacon; drain on paper towel, reserving drippings.
3. Brown onion and green pepper in 2 tablespoons bacon drippings.
4. Crumble bacon; add to beans along with onion, green pepper, seasonings and tomatoes.
5. Cover and simmer gently 15 minutes.

Green Bean Creole (Variation)

Use 2 packages (10 ounces each) frozen cut green beans instead of lima beans.

Eggplant Creole (Variation)

Use 1 medium-size eggplant, pared and cubed, instead of beans. Do not cook eggplant before combining with other ingredients. Increase salt to 1 teaspoon. Cook 15 to 20 minutes, or until eggplant is tender.

Lima Beans with Cheese

Serves 4

2 pounds lima beans, shelled
boiling salted water
½ teaspoon celery salt
¼ cup light cream

¼ teaspoon pepper
½ cup grated process
  American cheese
1 tablespoon butter, melted

1. Cook beans in a small amount of boiling salted water until tender; drain.
2. Mix beans with remaining ingredients; put in a 1-quart casserole.
3. Bake in preheated 350° F. oven 15 minutes, or until thoroughly heated.

Chili Limas

Serves 4

2 pounds lima beans, shelled
boiling salted water
1 small onion, minced

3 tablespoons butter or
  margarine
⅓ cup chili sauce

dash of cayenne

1. Cook beans in a small amount boiling salted water until tender.
2. Cook onion in butter until tender; add chili sauce and a dash of cayenne.
3. Drain beans; add sauce and heat well.

Favorite Lima Barbecue

Serves 4

1 package (10 ounces) frozen
   fordhook lima beans
¼ cup diced onion
dash of garlic powder
2 tablespoons corn oil
1 can (8 ounces) tomato sauce

3 tablespoons brown sugar
1½ tablespoons lemon juice
½ teaspoon dry mustard
¾ teaspoon salt
2 teaspoons original
   Worcestershire sauce

1. Cook lima beans according to package directions; drain.
2. Meanwhile, sauté onion and garlic powder in oil until onion is tender.
3. Stir in tomato sauce, brown sugar, lemon juice, mustard, salt and Worcestershire sauce; heat to a boil.
4. Reduce heat and simmer, uncovered, 15 minutes.
5. Add drained beans; simmer an additional 10 minutes, or until sauce is slightly thickened.

Elegant Mushroom Casserole

Serves 4

2 bouillon cubes (chicken
   or vegetarian)
¼ cup hot water
1 pound fresh mushrooms
2 tablespoons flour
½ cup heavy cream

½ teaspoon salt
dash of pepper
½ cup fine dry bread crumbs
½ cup freshly grated Parmesan
   cheese
¼ cup butter or margarine

1. Dissolve bouillon cubes in water in a small saucepan; cool.
2. Wash and slice mushrooms into a 2-quart casserole.
3. Stir flour into bouillon until smooth.
4. Add cream, salt and pepper; cook until thickened.
5. Pour cream sauce over mushrooms.
6. Mix crumbs and cheese; sprinkle over top.
7. Dot with butter; bake in preheated 350° F. oven 30 minutes, or until browned.

Marinated Mushrooms

Makes about 1 quart; serves 8

1 pound fresh mushrooms
6 tablespoons olive or
   vegetable oil
¾ cup dry white wine
1½ teaspoons salt
⅛ teaspoon cayenne pepper

¼ teaspoon dried leaf
   oregano
¼ cup chopped fresh parsley
2 tablespoons chopped
   fresh onion
3 tablespoons fresh lemon
   juice

1. Slice mushrooms; place in a glass or earthenware bowl and set aside.
2. Combine remaining ingredients in a saucepan; simmer 15 minutes.
3. Remove from heat; pour over mushrooms.
4. Cover and refrigerate several hours.

Steamed Mushrooms

Serves 4 to 6

1 pound medium-size mushrooms,
  washed and trimmed
1 teaspoon seasoned salt
⅛ teaspoon seasoned pepper

¼ teaspoon paprika
¼ cup butter or margarine
2 tablespoons dry sherry
¼ cup chopped parsley

1. Place mushrooms in the center of a 24 × 18-inch piece of heavy-duty foil.
2. Sprinkle with seasoned salt, seasoned pepper and paprika.
3. Dot with butter; sprinkle sherry over all.
4. Fold foil securely, leaving room for steam expansion; place in a shallow baking pan.
5. Bake in preheated 400° F. oven 20 minutes.
6. Before serving, sprinkle with parsley.

NOTE: This dish may be prepared on top of the barbecue.

Mushroom-Rice Ring Amandine

Serves 8

¼ cup butter or margarine
2½ cups (½ pound) sliced
  mushrooms
¾ cup chopped onions
1¾ cups uncooked processed
  rice
1 can (10¾ ounces) condensed
  chicken broth
2¾ cups water

1 tablespoon original
  Worcestershire sauce
½ teaspoon salt
⅓ cup toasted sliced almonds
¼ cup chopped parsley
2 packages (10 ounces each)
  frozen green peas, cooked
  and drained

1. Melt butter in a large skillet.
2. Add mushrooms and onions; sauté until tender, about 5 minutes.
3. Stir in rice, broth, water, Worcestershire sauce and salt; bring to a boil.
4. Reduce heat and simmer, covered, until rice is tender and liquid is absorbed, about 25 minutes.
5. Stir in almonds and parsley.
6. Pack into a buttered 6-cup ring mold.
7. Unmold onto a heated platter; fill center of ring with hot peas.

Mushroom-Parsley Stuffed Green Peppers

Serves 6

6 green peppers
boiling water
1½ teaspoons salt
¼ teaspoon minced garlic
¼ cup minced onion
4 cups toasted bread cubes

⅓ cup butter or margarine
4 cups diced fresh mushrooms
1 teaspoon fresh lemon juice
¾ teaspoon Italian seasoning
1½ cups finely chopped
  parsley

¼ cup heavy cream

1. Wash peppers; cut a thin slice from the stem end of each. Remove seeds.
2. Place peppers in a saucepan with boiling water to cover and 1 teaspoon salt; cover and bring to a boil.
3. Boil 5 minutes.
4. Remove peppers from water; invert on a tray to drain well.
5. Sauté garlic, onion and bread cubes in butter until onion is transparent and bread cubes are golden, about 8 minutes.
6. Add mushrooms and lemon juice; cook 2 to 3 minutes.
7. Stir in remaining salt, Italian seasoning, parsley and heavy cream.
8. Spoon into drained peppers.
9. Place peppers in a close-fitting casserole; cover and bake in preheated 375° F. oven 20 minutes.

Stewed Okra & Tomatoes

Serves 6

1 small onion, chopped
2 tablespoons corn oil
1 package (10 ounces) frozen
   okra

1 can (16 ounces) tomatoes
½ teaspoon salt
¼ teaspoon pepper

1. Cook onion in oil in a saucepan over moderate heat until golden.
2. Add remaining ingredients; cook until okra is tender and mixture thickens, 10 to 15 minutes, stirring occasionally to prevent sticking.

Onion Casserole

Serves 6 to 8

2 tablespoons butter or
   margarine
2 large Bermuda onions,
   peeled, sliced and separated
   into rings
½ pound Swiss cheese,
   grated (about 2 cups)

¼ teaspoon ground pepper
1 can (10 ¾ ounces) condensed
   cream of chicken soup
1 cup milk
8 slices buttered, slightly
   dry bread (amount of bread
   optional)

1. Melt butter in a large frying pan; add onions.
2. Cover and cook slowly over low heat, stirring often, 15 minutes, or until onions are soft.
3. Spoon onions into a 6-cup baking dish; spread cheese over top.
4. Sprinkle with pepper.
5. Heat together soup and milk in the same frying pan, stirring constantly until smooth.
6. Pour liquid over onion-cheese layer; stir lightly with tip of knife to let sauce flow to bottom of baking dish.
7. Overlap bread slices in ring on top.
8. Bake in preheated 350° F. oven 30 minutes, or until bread is toasted and sauce is bubbly.

Spicy Baked Onions
Serves 8

⅓ cup butter or margarine
1 tablespoon brown sugar
1½ teaspoons salt
¼ teaspoon ground nutmeg
⅛ teaspoon ground cayenne
  pepper
1⁄16 teaspoon ground cloves

1⁄16 teaspoon ground white
  pepper
2 dozen small white onions,
  peeled and parboiled
¼ cup blanched slivered
  almonds, toasted

1. Melt butter or margarine in a shallow baking dish.
2. Add brown sugar, salt and spices; mix well.
3. Add onions; stir until coated.
4. Cover dish and bake in preheated 375° F. oven 45 minutes, or until done, stirring every 15 minutes.
5. Sprinkle toasted almonds over the top.

Whipped Onions & Potatoes
Serves 4

3 onions
3 medium potatoes
boiling salted water

3 tablespoons butter
salt to taste
pepper to taste

1. Peel and quarter onions and potatoes.
2. Cook onions and potatoes in a small amount of boiling salted water until potatoes are tender.
3. Drain and mash.
4. Add butter, salt and pepper to taste; beat well.

Roasted Onions
Serves 8

2 packages (20 ounces each)
  frozen baby onions
4 teaspoons brown sugar
1 teaspoon seasoned salt
dash of seasoned pepper
2 tablespoons dry au jus
  gravy mix

½ cup water
½ cup white wine
3 tablespoons butter
2 tablespoons lemon juice
2 tablespoons chopped parsley

1. Place frozen onions in a 2-quart baking dish.
2. Add brown sugar, seasoned salt, seasoned pepper, gravy mix, water and wine; mix well.
3. Dot with butter.
4. Cover and bake in preheated 375° F. oven 45 minutes.
5. Uncover and bake 15 to 20 minutes longer, or until top is glazed.
6. Add lemon juice and parsley just before serving.

French-Fried Onion Rings

Serves 8 to 10

3 to 4 large Spanish onions
ice water
1 cup unsifted all-purpose
  flour

½ teaspoon salt
½ teaspoon baking soda
1 egg
1 cup buttermilk

peanut oil

1. Cut onions into ¼-inch-thick slices; separate slices into rings.
2. Soak rings in ice water at least 2 hours; drain and dry thoroughly.
3. Meanwhile, sift flour with salt and baking soda.
4. Beat egg; add buttermilk.
5. Add dry ingredients to egg mixture; beat until blended.
6. Dip onion rings in batter; fry in deep hot peanut oil heated to 375° F. until golden brown; drain on paper towels.

Fresh Parsnip Cakes

Serves 4

2 cups mashed cooked parsnips
1½ teaspoons salt
¼ teaspoon ground black
  pepper
1 teaspoon sugar

1 teaspoon paprika
1 teaspoon fresh lemon juice
1 egg
½ cup fine dry bread crumbs
flour

bacon drippings

1. Combine mashed parsnips, salt, black pepper, sugar, paprika, lemon juice, egg and bread crumbs; mix well.
2. Shape mixture into 2½-inch patties, ½-inch thick.
3. Dip patties in flour; sauté in bacon drippings, turning to brown both sides.
4. Serve hot.

Peas à la Crème

Serves 4

⅓ cup dairy sour cream
½ teaspoon instant chicken-
  flavored bouillon
½ teaspoon lemon juice

dash white pepper
1 can (16 ounces) peas
fresh dill (optional
  garnish)

1. Mix sour cream and bouillon in a saucepan; let stand 10 minutes to dissolve bouillon.
2. Add lemon juice and white pepper.
3. Place over low heat to blend flavors; do not boil.
4. Heat peas in their own liquid; drain.
5. Place peas in a serving dish; top with sauce.
6. Garnish with fresh dill if desired.

37

Dill-Sauced Peas

Serves 4

2 tablespoons butter or
margarine, melted
2 teaspoons cornstarch
1 teaspoon instant chicken-
flavored bouillon

¼ teaspoon onion salt
⅛ teaspoon white pepper
1 can (16 ounces) peas
½ cup dairy sour cream
½ teaspoon dill

1. Blend together butter, cornstarch, bouillon, onion salt and pepper in a saucepan.
2. Drain peas, reserving ¼ cup liquid.
3. Add reserved liquid to saucepan; stir until smooth.
4. Cook over moderate heat, stirring constantly, until slightly thickened.
5. Add sour cream and dill.
6. Stir in peas; heat to serving temperature but do not boil.

Quick Pea Medley

Serves 4

2 tablespoons butter or
margarine
¼ cup chopped onion
¼ cup chopped green pepper
1 package (10 ounces) frozen
peas

1 can (8¼ ounces) tomatoes,
broken up
1½ teaspoons original
Worcestershire sauce
½ teaspoon salt

1. Melt butter in a medium-size saucepan.
2. Add onion and green pepper; sauté 3 minutes.
3. Add peas, tomatoes, Worcestershire sauce and salt; mix gently.
4. Bring to a boil, reduce heat and simmer, uncovered, 5 minutes.

Cheese-Stuffed Potatoes

Serves 6

6 baking potatoes
corn oil
3 tablespoons butter or
margarine
¼ cup chopped onion

2 teaspoons original
Worcestershire sauce
½ teaspoon salt
¾ cup shredded sharp
Cheddar cheese

paprika (optional)

1. Brush potatoes lightly with oil; place on a baking sheet.
2. Bake in preheated 400° F. oven until potatoes are tender, about 1 hour.
3. Cut potatoes in half lengthwise; carefully scoop out potato from skins.
4. Mash potato with butter, onion, Worcestershire sauce and salt.
5. Spoon mashed potato mixture into potato shells; top with cheese.
6. Return to hot oven and bake until cheese is melted, about 15 minutes.
7. Sprinkle with paprika if desired.

Idaho Potato Skins with Parmesan Topping

Makes 16 wedges

4 Idaho potatoes
2 tablespoons butter or
margarine, melted

½ cup mayonnaise
2 tablespoons grated Parmesan
cheese

2 teaspoons grated onion

1. Wash potatoes; dry and prick with a fork.
2. Bake potatoes in preheated 425° F. oven 50 to 60 minutes, or until soft.
3. Cool potatoes slightly; cut into wedge-shaped quarters and scrape out pulp.
4. Place skins, skin-side down, on baking sheet; brush lightly with melted butter.
5. Return to oven; bake 10 minutes longer, or until crispy.
6. Combine mayonnaise, cheese and onion in a small bowl; mix well.
7. Spread topping on potato skins.
8. Place under broiler, 4 inches from heat; broil 2 to 3 minutes until topping is golden.
9. Serve hot.

Potatoes au Gratin

Serves 6

4 cups thinly sliced peeled
  potatoes
¾ cup minced onion
¾ teaspoon salt

1 can (10 ¾ ounces) condensed
  Cheddar cheese soup
½ cup milk
1 tablespoon original
  Worcestershire sauce

1. Arrange potatoes, onions and salt in alternate layers in a well-buttered 2-quart casserole.
2. Repeat three times.
3. Heat soup, milk and Worcestershire sauce in a saucepan; pour over potato mixture.
4. Cover and bake in preheated 375° F. oven 45 minutes.
5. Remove cover; bake 15 minutes longer.

Potato Patties

Serves 6

2 cups seasoned mashed
  potatoes
1 egg or 2 egg yolks,
  slightly beaten

1 tablespoon minced onion
1 tablespoon chopped green
  pepper
2 tablespoons corn oil

1. Combine all ingredients except oil; mix well.
2. Shape into 6 patties.
3. Brown well in oil, about 4 minutes on each side.

NOTE: Leftover mashed potatoes or instant mashed potatoes, prepared according to package directions, may be used in this recipe.

Hashed Brown O'Brien Potatoes

Serves 8

4 tablespoons butter
½ cup chopped onion
4 cups potatoes, boiled whole,
   cooled, then peeled and cut
   into ⅓-inch cubes

¼ cup green pepper (green
   part only), cut into slivers
   1-inch long
⅓ cup canned pimientos, cut
   into slivers 1-inch long
1 teaspoon salt
½ teaspoon pepper

1. Melt butter in a large skillet over medium heat.
2. Add onions; sauté until golden.
3. Add potatoes; sauté 5 minutes, stirring lightly with a fork.
4. Mix in green pepper, pimientos, salt and pepper with a fork; sauté 1 minute longer without stirring, or until brown on bottom, forming crust.
5. Turn mixture over with pancake turner; let other side brown, about 5 minutes.
6. Remove from pan with pancake turner; serve immediately.

Idaho Puff de Terre

Serves 4

1 package (3¼ ounces)
   instant mashed potatoes
2 eggs, separated

2 cans (4½ ounces each)
   deviled ham
1 cup shredded Cheddar cheese

3 tablespoons chopped chives

1. Prepare mashed potatoes according to package directions, omitting butter and reducing salt to ¼ teaspoon.
2. Beat egg yolks in a small bowl; stir in ham, cheese, chives and prepared mashed potatoes.
3. In the small bowl of electric mixer, beat egg whites until stiff; gently fold into potato mixture.
4. Spoon mixture into four buttered 10-ounce custard cups or individual soufflé dishes.
5. Bake in preheated 375° F. oven 30 minutes, or until golden brown.

Potato 'n Broccoli Supreme

Serves 8

3 cups hot mashed potatoes
   (5 to 6 medium potatoes)
1 package (3 ounces) cream
   cheese, softened
¼ cup milk
1 egg
2 tablespoons margarine
salt to taste

pepper to taste
1 can (2.8 ounces) French-fried
   onions
2 packages (10 ounces each)
   frozen broccoli spears,
   cooked and drained
1 cup (4 ounces) shredded
   American cheese

1. Whip together potatoes, cream cheese, milk, egg and margarine until smooth; season to taste with salt and pepper.
2. Fold in half the can of French-fried onions.
3. Spread potato mixture over bottom and up sides of a buttered 8 × 12-inch baking dish to form a shell.
4. Bake, uncovered, in preheated 350° F. oven 25 to 30 minutes.
5. Arrange hot broccoli spears in potato shell; sprinkle with cheese and remaining onions.
6. Bake, uncovered, 5 minutes longer.

Stuffed Baked Potatoes

Serves 6

6 medium-size baking potatoes
1 package (3 ounces) cream
   cheese, at room temperature

⅓ cup milk
1 teaspoon salt
⅓ cup butter or margarine

paprika

1. Rub potatoes with a little butter if soft skins are desired.
2. Bake in preheated 425° F. oven 50 to 60 minutes, or until potatoes are soft when pressed.
3. Slash tops lengthwise and crosswise; fold back flaps, scoop out inside and mash thoroughly.
4. Soften cream cheese; blend in milk, salt and butter until smooth and creamy.
5. Add cream cheese mixture gradually to hot mashed potatoes, blending thoroughly.
6. Stuff skins with potato mixture; sprinkle with paprika.
7. Return to oven a few minutes to brown tops.

Lacy Potato Fritters

Makes about 3 dozen fritters

2 eggs
1 clove garlic, minced
1 tablespoon soy sauce
1 tablespoon sesame seeds

1 tablespoon flour
1 tablespoon baking powder
3 Idaho potatoes, peeled
corn oil for frying

1. Beat eggs in a large mixing bowl; stir in garlic, soy sauce, sesame seeds, flour and baking powder.
2. Grate potatoes coarsely, using large holes of hand grater or food processor.
3. Squeeze out as much liquid as possible from potatoes.
4. Stir potatoes into egg batter.
5. Heat 2 inches oil to 325° F. in an electric frypan or deep fryer.
6. Drop a forkful of potato mixture into hot oil. (Mixture should spread to make a lacy effect.)
7. Brown quickly on one side; turn with fork and brown other side.
8. Drain on paper towels.
9. Repeat with remaining potato mixture.

41

Hot Pumpkin Soup

Serves 6

1 cup mashed cooked pumpkin
2½ cups chicken broth
1 tablespoon flour
1 teaspoon salt
⅛ teaspoon ground ginger
⅛ teaspoon ground nutmeg

1 tablespoon minced onion
1 cup half and half or
  evaporated milk
2 large eggs, beaten
chopped fresh parsley or
  fresh chives (for garnish)

1. Combine pumpkin and chicken broth in a saucepan.
2. Mix together flour, salt, ginger, nutmeg and onion.
3. Blend in ¼ cup half and half to make a smooth paste.
4. Gradually add remaining half and half and eggs; stir into pumpkin mixture.
5. Cook 10 minutes over low heat, stirring constantly.
6. Serve hot, garnished with chopped parsley.

Radish & Tomato Salad

Serves 4 to 6

1 large tomato
2 bunches radishes
1 teaspoon chopped fresh mint
1 tablespoon minced onion
2 tablespoons fresh lemon
  juice

2 tablespoons olive or
  salad oil
1 teaspoon salt
¼ teaspoon ground black
  pepper
¼ teaspoon sugar

lettuce (optional)

1. Peel tomato and dice finely.
2. Wash radishes; cut off green tops and roots.
3. Slice radishes thinly; add to tomatoes.
4. Combine remaining ingredients; pour over vegetables.
5. Serve on lettuce, if desired, or as a relish on the dinner plate.

Rutabaga & Potato Provençale

Serves 8 to 10

4 cups (2 pounds) peeled,
  diced rutabagas
4 cups (2 to 2½ pounds)
  peeled, diced potatoes
1 teaspoon salt

1 teaspoon sugar
1 inch boiling water
¼ cup butter or margarine
¼ teaspoon ground black
  pepper

1 tablespoon minced onion

1. Place rutabagas, potatoes, salt, sugar and enough boiling water to a depth of 1 inch in a saucepan.
2. Bring to a boil; boil, uncovered, 5 minutes.
3. Cover and continue cooking 20 minutes, or until vegetables are tender.
4. Remove cover and cook vegetables over low heat 15 minutes to evaporate water.
5. Add butter or margarine, black pepper and onion; mix well.
6. Turn into an ovenproof serving dish or casserole; rough top with a spoon.
7. Bake in preheated 350° F. oven 30 minutes.

Baked Soybeans

Serves 6

2 cups dried soybeans
6 cups water
1 teaspoon salt
¼ pound bacon, diced
½ cup chopped onion

¼ cup brown sugar, packed
1 teaspoon dry mustard
¾ cup bean cooking liquid
  plus water
¼ cup molasses

1. Sort soybeans to remove any discolored or cracked or shriveled beans.
2. Soak in salted water 10 minutes.
3. Bring to a boil; boil 2 minutes.
4. Remove from heat and let stand 1 hour.
5. Simmer, covered, in soaking water 2 to 3 hours, or until beans are tender. (Add water, if necessary, during cooking.)
6. Drain beans, reserving cooking liquid.
7. Place soybeans in a greased beanpot or 2-quart casserole.
8. Add remaining ingredients; stir into soybeans.
9. Cover and bake in preheated 325° F. oven 3 hours.
10. Remove cover during last hour of baking to reduce liquid and brown top.

Creamed Spinach Ring

Serves 6

2 packages (10 ounces each)
  frozen chopped spinach
2 tablespoons butter or
  margarine
2 tablespoons chopped onion
2 tablespoons all-purpose flour
2 eggs, separated
3 cans (10¾ ounces each)
  condensed cream of mushroom
  soup, undiluted

⅓ cup half and half
½ teaspoon nutmeg
salt to taste
pepper to taste
1 hard-cooked egg (for garnish)
1 jar (2 ounces) sliced
  pimientos, drained (for
  garnish)

1. Cook spinach according to package directions; drain and squeeze excess moisture from spinach.
2. Melt butter; add onion and sauté until transparent.
3. Stir in flour, beaten egg yolks, ⅓ cup undiluted soup and the half and half, stirring constantly.
4. Add spinach, nutmeg, salt and pepper; cook, stirring occasionally, until thickened.
5. Cool.
6. Meanwhile, beat egg whites until stiff peaks form; carefully fold into cooled spinach mixture.
7. Turn into a greased 4-cup ring mold; set mold in a pan of hot water.
8. Bake in preheated 325° F. oven 50 minutes, or until set.
9. Carefully invert spinach ring onto heated platter.
10. Warm remaining undiluted soup; fill center of ring mold with heated soup.
11. Garnish soup with chopped hard-cooked egg.
12. Garnish spinach ring with pimientos.

Spinach Balls

Makes about 60 appetizers

2 packages (10 ounces each)
    frozen chopped spinach
2 medium-size onions, chopped
6 eggs, unbeaten
2 cups herb-seasoned
    stuffing mix

½ cup grated Parmesan cheese
¼ cup butter or margarine,
    melted
1 teaspoon salt
1 tablespoon garlic salt
½ teaspoon thyme

pepper to taste

1. Thaw spinach; place in a large sieve.
2. Drain spinach thoroughly, squeezing out as much water as possible.
3. Add spinach to remaining ingredients; mix well.
4. Shape mixture into balls the size of walnuts.
5. Preheat oven to 350° F.; bake in preheated greased jelly-roll pan 20 minutes.
6. Serve promptly.

NOTE: Spinach balls may be wrapped and frozen, then thawed 1 hour before baking.

Spinach with Sesame Dressing

Serves 4 to 6

1 pound spinach
water

3 tablespoons sesame seeds
3 tablespoons soy sauce

2 tablespoons Sake

1. Wash spinach, leaving stems intact.
2. Boil spinach in a small amount of water 3 minutes, keeping stems together.
3. Toast sesame seeds in a heavy skillet until they brown and pop; grind briefly in an electric blender.
4. Add soy sauce; grind again briefly.
5. Add Sake; mix well.
6. Press excess water out of cooked spinach; cut into 1½-inch lengths.
7. Toss spinach lightly with soy-sesame dressing until coated.
8. Serve in small individual bowls.

NOTE: Cooked cauliflower or cabbage may be prepared in the same manner.

Spinach Soufflé

Serves 6

1 package (10 ounces) frozen
    chopped spinach
1 tablespoon minced onion
¼ cup corn oil
⅓ cup flour

1½ cups milk
1 teaspoon salt
¼ teaspoon pepper
4 eggs, separated
½ teaspoon cream of tartar

1. Cook spinach as directed on package, but omit salt; drain.
2. Lightly brown onion in oil in a heavy 1-quart saucepan; blend in flour.
3. Slowly stir in milk; bring to a boil, stirring constantly.
4. Reduce heat, and cook 1 minute longer, stirring constantly.
5. Add salt, pepper and spinach.
6. Beat egg yolks slightly; stir in a little hot mixture.
7. Stir egg yolks into remaining hot mixture; cook 1 minute longer.
8. Cool slightly.
9. Add cream of tartar to egg whites; beat until stiff but not dry.
10. Fold spinach mixture into egg whites.
11. Pour into greased 2-quart casserole; set casserole in a pan of hot water.
12. Bake in preheated 350° F. oven 1¼ hours. (Soufflé is done when a knife inserted in center comes out clean.)

Fresh Spinach Ring with Shredded Beets

Serves 8

2 pounds fresh spinach, uncooked
3 tablespoons butter or
 margarine
½ teaspoon salt
½ teaspoon sugar

⅛ teaspoon ground black
 pepper
1 teaspoon chopped onion
2 eggs, well beaten
Shredded Beets

1. Cook washed spinach in a covered saucepan, without water, over low heat until done; chop fine.
2. Add remaining ingredients except Shredded Beets to spinach.
3. Pack into a buttered 8-inch ring mold; set in pan of hot water.
4. Bake in preheated 350° F. oven 25 to 30 minutes, or until firm.
5. Unmold onto a large serving plate.

Shredded Beets

3 cups shredded raw beets
¼ cup boiling water
½ teaspoon salt

1 tablespoon fresh lemon juice
1 tablespoon butter or
 margarine

1. Cook beets in boiling water in a covered saucepan until tender, about 5 minutes.
2. Add remaining ingredients.
3. Spoon into center of spinach ring.

Fresh Spinach Slaw with Dill Sauce

Serves 4

2 cups finely shredded cabbage
1 cup finely shredded fresh
 spinach
2 teaspoons minced onion
½ teaspoon salt

⅛ teaspoon freshly ground
 black pepper
2 teaspoons lemon juice
1 tablespoon mayonnaise
¼ teaspoon crushed dill seed

Combine all ingredients; toss lightly.

Fresh Spinach-Filled Artichokes

Serves 4

1 package (10 ounces) fresh
  spinach
water
2 tablespoons chopped fresh
  onion
1 small clove garlic, minced
2 tablespoons melted butter or
  margarine

2 tablespoons flour
1 teaspoon salt
few grains of pepper
⅔ cup milk
½ cup sliced fresh carrots,
  cooked
4 cooked artichokes

1. Wash spinach; cook in water clinging to leaves in covered saucepan until just wilted. Drain, if necessary.
2. Chop spinach fine; set aside.
3. Sauté onion and garlic in butter or margarine until tender.
4. Blend in flour, salt and pepper.
5. Gradually stir in milk; cook over medium heat, stirring constantly, until mixture reaches its boiling point.
6. Stir in spinach and carrots.
7. Fill artichokes with spinach mixture.

Spinach & Endive Salad

Serves 6

1 clove garlic, cut in half
¼ cup olive or salad oil
1 bunch curly endive
¼ pound fresh raw spinach

¾ teaspoon dried leaf oregano
½ teaspoon salt
⅛ teaspoon pepper
1 tablespoon wine vinegar

1 tablespoon fresh lemon juice

1. Add garlic to oil; let stand 1 hour.
2. Remove garlic from oil; rub garlic over inside of wooden salad bowl.
3. Wash and dry endive and spinach thoroughly; tear into bite-size pieces and place in salad bowl.
4. Add remaining ingredients to garlic oil; pour over salad.
5. Toss lightly and serve.

Golden Emerald Baked Squash

Serves 4

1 medium-size yellow summer
  squash, sliced ¼-inch thick
1 medium zucchini, sliced
  ¼-inch thick
¼ cup butter or margarine,
  melted

½ cup coarsely chopped
  walnuts
½ cup grated Parmesan cheese
2 tablespoons chopped fresh
  dill or 2 teaspoons dried
  dill

1. Arrange half the squash and zucchini slices in a 9-inch pie plate; brush with melted butter.
2. Combine walnuts, cheese and dill in a small bowl; sprinkle half the mixture over squash.
3. Repeat with remaining ingredients.
4. Bake in preheated 350° F. oven 25 to 30 minutes, or until squash is tender.

NOTE: Recipe may be assembled in advance. Cover and refrigerate, then bake.

Spaghetti Squash with Tomato Sauce

Serves 4 to 6

1 medium onion, minced
1 clove garlic, crushed
½ pound lean ground beef, crumbled
2 tablespoons olive oil (optional)
4 cups cut ripe or canned tomatoes, undrained

1 tablespoon tomato paste
½ teaspoon dried basil
½ teaspoon oregano
salt to taste
pepper to taste
1 spaghetti squash, 3 pounds, boiled (page 60)
grated Parmesan cheese

1. Sauté onions, garlic and ground beef with oil, if desired, in a skillet until meat is browned.
2. Add tomatoes with liquid, tomato paste and seasonings; simmer, uncovered, 30 to 45 minutes, stirring occasionally.
3. Pull cooked squash strands out with a fork onto a platter; top with sauce and cheese.

Squash Sauté

Serves 6

2 tablespoons olive or corn oil
½ pound cooked ham, cut into strips
1 cup diced green pepper
2 scallions, cut in 1-inch pieces

1 cup fresh pea pods
2 large tomatoes, seeded and chopped
2 medium zucchini, sliced
¼ teaspoon dried leaf thyme
¼ teaspoon salt

3 tablespoons grated Parmesan cheese

1. Heat oil in a large skillet; sauté ham until slightly browned.
2. Remove ham from skillet; set aside.
3. Sauté green pepper and scallions 3 minutes; add pea pods, tomatoes, zucchini, thyme and salt.
4. Continue to cook over medium heat until vegetables are crisp-tender.
5. Return ham to skillet; heat through.
6. Transfer to serving dish; sprinkle with grated cheese.

Southern-Style Squash Casserole

Serves 8

2 slices bacon, crumbled
½ cup chopped onion
½ cup chopped green pepper
2 cups cooked squash
1 cup diced sharp Cheddar
   cheese
½ teaspoon celery seed

2 eggs, well beaten
3 tablespoons chopped
   pimiento
3 tablespoons melted butter
salt to taste
pepper to taste
½ cup hot milk

1 cup cracker crumbs

1. Brown bacon; crumble and set aside, reserving bacon fat.
2. Sauté onions in bacon fat until transparent.
3. Add green pepper to same pan; sauté lightly a few minutes longer.
4. Turn mixture into a bowl; add all remaining ingredients except crumbs.
5. Place in greased 6 × 12-inch heatproof casserole; top with crumbs.
6. Bake in preheated 350° F. oven 30 to 35 minutes.

Fresh Squash Chips

Serves 4

1 butternut squash
ice water

corn oil for deep-fat frying
salt

ground ginger

1. Peel and seed squash; slice tissue-paper thin with vegetable parer, as for potato chips.
2. Soak slices in ice water for 1 hour; drain and pat dry.
3. Fry in hot deep oil heated to 380° F. until brown; drain on paper towel.
4. Sprinkle with salt and ground ginger.

Boiled Spaghetti Squash

Serves 4 to 6

Split squash (weighing about 3 pounds), using a heavy knife. Scoop out seeds. Place, cut-side down, in a wide pan with 2 to 3 inches of water. Cover and steam 20 minutes, or bake split squash 45 minutes in pan in preheated 350° F. oven, or microwave 8 to 15 minutes on HIGH, cut-side up, in a dish with a few tablespoons of water. Pull out cooked strands with a fork. Serve buttered and seasoned, or with a zesty tomato sauce.

Sweet Potato Casserole Supreme

Serves 6 to 8

3 cups sweet potatoes
½ cup sugar
½ cup butter

2 eggs, beaten
1 teaspoon vanilla
⅓ cup milk

Topping

1. Boil and mash potatoes.
2. Mix in sugar, butter, eggs, vanilla and milk.
3. Put in baking dish; add topping.
4. Follow final step below.

Topping

⅓ cup butter, melted
1 cup light brown sugar

½ cup flour
1 cup chopped nuts

Combine all ingredients and spread over sweet potato mixture. Bake 25 minutes in preheated 350° F. oven 30 minutes, or until nuts are golden.

Sweet Potato Gingerbread

Serves 8

1 cup sifted all-purpose flour
2 teaspoons baking powder
1 teaspoon ground ginger
¾ teaspoon ground cloves
½ teaspoon salt
⅓ cup butter or margarine

1 cup mashed fresh sweet
   potatoes, cooled
½ cup sugar
¼ teaspoon baking soda
2 eggs
½ cup light molasses

1. Sift together flour, baking powder, ginger, cloves and salt; set aside.
2. Combine butter and sweet potatoes; mix well.
3. Add sugar and soda; stir until thoroughly blended.
4. Beat in eggs, one at a time.
5. Add flour mixture alternately with molasses; mix well.
6. Turn batter into greased 8 × 8 × 2-inch baking pan.
7. Bake in preheated 350° F. oven 1 hour, or until done.
8. Cool in pan 10 minutes before turning out on wire rack to cool.

Sweet Potatoes in Orange Shells

Serves 6

3 oranges
1 can (16 ounces) sweet
   potatoes, undrained
2 tablespoons butter or
   margarine, melted

3 tablespoons brown sugar,
   packed
½ teaspoon salt
¼ cup flaked coconut
6 miniature marshmallows

1. Squeeze oranges; reserve juice.
2. Remove membranes from orange shells.
3. Mash sweet potatoes in their liquid; blend in 3 tablespoons orange juice, butter, brown sugar and salt.
4. Stir in coconut.
5. Spoon sweet potato mixture into orange shells; place in shallow baking pan.
6. Bake in preheated 350° F. oven 20 to 30 minutes, or until lightly browned on top.
7. Top with marshmallows; bake 5 minutes longer to melt and brown marshmallows.

Fresh Cranberry & Sweet Potato Pudding

Serves 4 to 6

3 cups (1¾ pounds) mashed
   sweet potatoes
½ cup butter or margarine
¼ teaspoon salt

2 teaspoons grated orange
   rind
¾ cup sugar
2 cups fresh cranberries

½ cup fresh orange juice

1. Combine sweet potatoes, ¼ cup butter, salt and orange rind.
2. Blend in ¼ cup sugar and remaining butter.
3. Cook cranberries, remaining sugar and orange juice in a covered saucepan until skins pop.
4. Put mixture through a strainer.
5. Add strained mixture to potato mixture; mix well.
6. Turn into a buttered 1½-quart casserole.
7. Bake in preheated 375° F. oven 30 minutes, or until done.

NOTE: Serve with poultry, pork or veal.

Candied Sweet Potatoes

Serves 12

1 cup dark corn syrup
½ cup firmly packed dark
   brown sugar
2 tablespoons margarine

12 medium sweet potatoes,
   cooked, peeled and halved
   lengthwise

1. Bring corn syrup, brown sugar and margarine to a boil over medium heat in a small saucepan; reduce heat and simmer 5 minutes.
2. Pour ½ cup syrup into 13 × 9 × 2-inch baking dish.
3. Arrange potatoes in syrup; top with remaining syrup.
4. Bake in preheated 350° F. oven, basting often, 20 minutes, or until well glazed.

Baked Stuffed Sweet Potatoes

Serves 4

4 medium sweet potatoes
¼ cup light corn syrup

¼ cup margarine, melted
½ teaspoon salt

dash of ground cinnamon

1. Pierce each potato once with a fork; place on a cookie sheet.
2. Bake in preheated 400° F. oven 1 hour, or until tender.
3. Cut an oval in the top of each potato with a sharp knife; scoop out potatoes; reserving skins.
4. Mash potatoes in a bowl.
5. Add corn syrup, margarine and salt; stir until smooth.
6. Spoon potato mixture into skins; sprinkle with cinnamon.
7. Bake in preheated 350° F. oven 15 minutes, or until heated through.

Savory Scalloped Tomatoes

Serves 8

3 tablespoons butter or
margarine
1 cup diced celery
½ cup chopped onion
2 tablespoons flour
1 can (1 pound 12 ounces)
tomatoes

4 teaspoons original
Worcestershire sauce
1 tablespoon sugar
1 teaspoon salt
4 slices toasted white
bread

1. Melt 2 tablespoons butter in a saucepan.
2. Add celery and onion; cook until tender, about 5 minutes.
3. Blend in flour; cook and stir 1 minute.
4. Remove from heat; stir in tomatoes (do not crush), Worcestershire sauce, sugar and salt.
5. Spread toast with remaining butter; cut into ½-inch cubes.
6. Stir half the bread cubes into tomato mixture; turn into a buttered 1½-quart casserole.
7. Bake, uncovered, in preheated 350° F. oven 30 minutes.
8. Top with remaining bread cubes; bake 10 to 12 minutes longer.

Helen's Green Tomato-Apple Pie

Serves 6

2 cups skinned, quartered
and thinly sliced green
tomatoes
boiling water
3 cups thin, peeled apple
slices
⅔ cup brown sugar,
firmly packed

⅓ cup granulated sugar
2½ cups flour
½ teaspoon cinnamon
⅛ teaspoon salt
pastry for two-crust pie
2 tablespoons butter or
margarine

1. To peel tomatoes easily, place in boiling water 2 to 3 minutes, or until skins can easily be slipped off.
2. Combine tomatoes, apples, sugars, flour, cinnamon and salt.
3. Place in a pastry-lined 9-inch pie pan; dot with butter.
4. Adjust top crust and flute edges; cut steam vents.
5. Bake in preheated 425° F. oven 50 to 60 minutes.

Broiled Tomatoes

Serves 4

4 tomatoes, halved
½ cup fine dry bread crumbs
¼ cup melted butter

2 teaspoons original
Worcestershire sauce

1. Place tomato halves under preheated broiler; broil 3 minutes.
2. Combine remaining ingredients; sprinkle over tomatoes.
3. Broil 3 minutes longer.

Tomato-Zucchini Casserole

Serves 4

1½ teaspoons chili powder
1 tablespoon parsley flakes, divided
½ teaspoon garlic powder
½ teaspoon onion powder
⅛ teaspoon salt
⅛ teaspoon ground black pepper

3 cups thinly sliced fresh zucchini
1 pound fresh tomatoes, sliced
¼ cup fresh white bread crumbs
1 tablespoon corn oil

1. Combine chili powder, 1½ teaspoons parsley flakes, garlic and onion powders, salt and black pepper in a small bowl.
2. In a lightly greased 6-cup casserole, place half the zucchini and half the tomatoes; sprinkle with half the seasoning mixture.
3. Repeat layers.
4. Combine bread crumbs, oil and remaining parsley flakes; sprinkle over vegetables.
5. Bake, uncovered, in preheated 375° F. oven about 40 minutes, or until vegetables are tender.

Wine-Glazed Tomatoes

Serves 6 to 8

3 tablespoons butter or margarine
1 tablespoon sugar
½ teaspoon seasoned salt

¼ cup rosé wine
4 large beefsteak tomatoes, cut into ⅜-inch slices
seasoned pepper to taste

1 teaspoon basil leaves

1. Melt butter in a large skillet over medium heat.
2. Add sugar, salt and wine; cook and stir until sugar melts, 4 minutes.
3. Place tomato slices in a single layer in skillet; sauté on high heat 2 minutes on each side, or until tender.
4. Arrange on serving plates; sprinkle with seasoned pepper and basil.

Tomato-Zucchini Parmesan

Serves 8 to 10

1 can (8 ounces) tomato sauce
1 can (16 ounces) tomato paste
¾ cup finely chopped onion
2 teaspoons Italian herb seasoning
1 clove garlic, minced or pressed
¼ teaspoon salt

1½ pounds zucchini, sliced ¼-inch thick
4 medium-size fresh California tomatoes, cored and sliced
½ cup Parmesan cheese
8 ounces Monterey Jack cheese, sliced

1. Combine tomato sauce, tomato paste, onion, Italian herb seasoning, garlic and salt in a medium-size saucepan; bring to a boil.
2. Reduce heat and simmer 15 minutes, stirring occasionally.
3. In a 13 × 9-inch pan, layer half of each: zucchini, tomatoes, sauce and Parmesan cheese.
4. Repeat layers.
5. Place Monterey Jack cheese on top; cover with aluminum foil.
6. Bake in preheated 375° F. oven 40 to 45 minutes, or until zucchini is tender.

Raw Turnip Salad

Serves 6

3 cups turnips, cut into
  julienne strips
½ teaspoon salt
2 tablespoons cider vinegar
1½ tablespoons salad oil
3 tablespoons soy sauce
1 teaspoon sugar

2 cups unpeeled, firm eating
  apples, cut into julienne
  strips
1 tablespoon toasted sesame
  seeds
shredded red or green pepper
  (for garnish)

1. Sprinkle turnips with salt; let stand 15 minutes.
2. Squeeze out excess liquid.
3. Combine vinegar, salad oil, soy sauce and sugar; add to turnips.
4. Add apples and sesame seeds; toss lightly.
5. Serve cold, garnished with shredded red or green pepper.

Grilled Garlic & Vegetables

Serves 8

8 whole heads fresh garlic
2 artichokes, trimmed and
  quartered
4 ears corn, halved crosswise
2 carrots, cut in
  1-inch chunks
2 zucchini, cut in
  1-inch chunks

1 cup butter or margarine
8 sprigs fresh rosemary or
  4 teaspoons dried
½ cup sliced almonds
salt to taste
pepper to taste

1. Peel outer skin from garlic bulbs, keeping cloves intact.
2. On a double thickness of heavy-duty aluminum foil, place one whole head of garlic, one artichoke quarter, one halved ear of corn and one-eighth of the carrot and zucchini chunks.
3. Dot with 2 tablespoons butter.
4. Top with a sprig of fresh rosemary and 1 tablespoon almonds; sprinkle with salt and pepper.
5. Fold up foil and seal tightly.
6. Repeat to make 8 single-serving packets.
7. Cook over hot coals, turning occasionally, 40 to 45 minutes.

Pasta & Mixed Vegetables

Serves 4 to 6

½ pound small, shell-style
   pasta
½ cup plus 1 tablespoon
   olive oil, divided
2 cloves garlic, finely
   minced
1 green pepper, cut in
   julienne strips
1 red pepper, cut in
   julienne strips

1 medium zucchini, sliced
2 cans (6½ or 7 ounces each)
   tuna, drained
½ cup chopped fresh parsley
¼ cup capers, drained
1 teaspoon dried leaf thyme
1 cup halved cherry tomatoes
½ cup small, black
   Provençale-style olives

1. Prepare pasta according to package directions; drain.
2. Toss pasta with 1 tablespoon olive oil.
3. Heat remaining olive oil in a large skillet; sauté garlic, green and red pepper and zucchini until tender.
4. Stir in tuna, parsley, capers and thyme; cook until heated through.
5. Toss pasta with tuna mixture in a large bowl.
6. Just before serving, add cherry tomatoes and olives.

Marinated Vegetable Salad

Serves 6 to 8

1 cup bottled Italian salad
   dressing
3 tablespoons original
   Worcestershire sauce
1 package (10 ounces) frozen
   cauliflower, cooked and
   drained

1 package (9 ounces) frozen cut
   green beans, cooked and
   drained
2 cups sliced zucchini
1 green pepper, cut into strips
1 red pepper, cut into strips

1 can (3½ ounces) pitted ripe olives, drained

1. Combine salad dressing and Worcestershire sauce; set aside.
2. Combine cauliflower, green beans, zucchini, green pepper, red pepper and olives in a large bowl.
3. Pour salad dressing over vegetables; toss well.
4. Cover and refrigerate until chilled, about 1 hour, stirring occasionally.

Five-Vegetable Salad

Serves 4 to 6

2 packages (10 ounces each)
   frozen mixed vegetables
½ cup coarsely chopped onion
6 tablespoons oil
3 tablespoons cider vinegar

1½ teaspoons original
   Worcestershire sauce
¾ teaspoon salt
⅛ teaspoon coarsely ground
   black pepper

⅛ teaspoon sugar

1. Cook vegetables in unsalted water, following package directions; drain.
2. Stir in onion.
3. Combine remaining ingredients; mix well.
4. Pour dressing over mixed vegetables; cover and refrigerate at least 12 hours before serving, stirring occasionally.

Vegetable Quiche

Serves 6

2 small zucchini (½ pound), thinly sliced

1 scallion, sliced

1 clove garlic, minced

¼ cup butter or margarine

1 medium tomato, peeled and chopped (about 1 cup)

½ cup chopped green pepper

¾ teaspoon salt or to taste

¼ teaspoon pepper

¼ teaspoon basil

¼ teaspoon thyme

1 can (16 ounces) bean sprouts, drained, rinsed and coarsely chopped

9-inch pastry shell, partially baked, or unbaked and brushed with egg white, then dried

3 eggs

¼ cup half and half

½ cup Parmesan cheese

1. Sauté zucchini, scallion and garlic in butter 5 minutes, stirring occasionally.
2. Stir in tomato, green pepper, salt, pepper, basil and thyme; cook over low heat 10 to 15 minutes, or until vegetables are tender and liquid has evaporated.
3. Mix bean sprouts into cooked vegetables; spread evenly in pastry shell.
4. Beat eggs and half and half until mixed but not frothy; pour over vegetables.
5. Sprinkle with Parmesan cheese.
6. Bake in preheated 375° F. oven 30 to 35 minutes, or until knife inserted near center comes out clean.
7. Serve hot or cold.

Frozen Vegetables Cooked in a Packet

Cooking frozen vegetables in aluminum foil is a great way to save energy. Vegetables can cook in the oven along with a roast, stew or casserole. Since there is no pan to wash, clean-up is a breeze, and vegetables retain food value because little or no moisture is added. The suggested temperature for cooking frozen vegetables in foil is 400° F., but you can adjust cooking time when you add your packet to an oven set at a lower temperature. Place vegetables on a large sheet of heavy-duty aluminum foil; add 2 tablespoons of water, 1 tablespoon butter or margarine, salt and pepper to taste, and your favorite seasoning.

To make a packet: Bring long ends of foil together and fold over vegetables; crimp ends to form an airtight packet. We suggest you place the packet in a shallow baking dish in case the foil develops a leak. Most frozen vegetables require 45 minutes to 1 hour cooking time. Cooking in a packet is also an ideal method to use when you are cooking out of doors. Follow the same instructions, placing the packet on the grill. Be sure the flames do not touch the foil, and be sure the coals are hot and glowing before you start to cook.

Oriental Salad

Serves 8

1 package (16 ounces) Japanese
   vegetables (contains French-
   cut green beans, broccoli,
   mushrooms, red peppers)
2 cups sliced celery
½ cup sliced water chestnuts
¼ cup sliced green onions
¼ cup oil

4 teaspoons soy sauce
1 teaspoon lemon juice
½ teaspoon salt
½ teaspoon ginger
⅛ teaspoon pepper
2 tablespoons sliced
   pimientos (for garnish)

1. Cook vegetables half the required time on package directions; drain.
2. Combine cooked vegetables, celery, water chestnuts and green onions in a large bowl.
3. Combine remaining ingredients except pimiento.
4. Pour over vegetable mixture; toss well.
5. Cover and chill at least 1 hour before serving; garnish with pimiento.

Baked Vegetable Macédoine

Serves 8 to 10

1 package (10 ounces) frozen
   mixed vegetables, thawed
1 package (10 ounces) frozen
   cauliflower, thawed
1 yellow squash, thinly
   sliced
1 zucchini, thinly
   sliced
1 potato, peeled and diced

1 cup cherry tomatoes, halved
½ cup chopped red onion
1 cup water
¼ cup oil
2 tablespoons original
   Worcestershire sauce
1 beef bouillon cube
2 large cloves garlic,
   crushed

½ teaspoon Italian seasoning

1. Place all vegetables in an ungreased 11 × 7 × 1½-inch baking pan; toss gently and set aside.
2. Combine remaining ingredients in a small saucepan; bring to a boil, stirring to dissolve bouillon cube.
3. Pour liquid over vegetables; cover tightly.
4. Bake in preheated 350° F. oven until vegetables are crisp-tender, about 1 hour, stirring once.

Vegetarian Fettucine

Serves 6 to 8

¼ cup butter
1 large eggplant, peeled and
   cut into 1-inch cubes
½ pound mushrooms, sliced
1 cup chopped onion
1½ pounds green beans,
   cut-up and cooked

1 cup bottled creamy-style
   Italian dressing
¾ cup half and half
½ cup grated Parmesan cheese
½ pound uncooked fettucine
   or egg noodles
1 teaspoon minced parsley

1. Melt butter in a large skillet; add eggplant, mushrooms and onion.
2. Cook, covered, stirring occasionally, 30 minutes, or until tender.
3. Add green beans and Italian dressing blended with half and half and cheese; heat through but do not boil.
4. Cook noodles according to package directions; drain.
5. Toss hot noodles with hot vegetable mixture; sprinkle with parsley.

NOTE: *This is an interesting dish made with green noodles (spinach noodles), available in supermarkets or gourmet shops.*

Milano Medley

Serves 6

1 package (16 ounces) frozen vegetables milano (contains carrots, cauliflower, green beans, zucchini and butter beans)	1 tablespoon instant minced onion
	¾ teaspoon salt
	½ teaspoon garlic salt
	dash of pepper
1 cup water	¼ cup white vinegar
2 tablespoons corn oil	2 medium-size tomatoes, quartered
4 teaspoons cornstarch	
1 tablespoon sugar	¼ cup walnut pieces

spaghetti noodles, cooked

1. Cook vegetables in ½ cup water 8 to 9 minutes; drain and set aside.
2. Combine ½ cup water, oil, cornstarch, sugar, onion, salt, garlic salt, pepper and vinegar in a medium-size skillet; cook, stirring constantly, until thickened.
3. Add reserved vegetables, tomatoes and walnuts; stir until coated with sauce.
4. Cover and cook until heated through, 1 to 2 minutes.
5. Serve over spaghetti noodles.

Vegetable-Mushroom Stew

Serves 4

¾ pound mushrooms	2 ¾ cups sliced zucchini
2 tablespoons corn oil	2 green peppers, seeded and cut into 1-inch pieces
½ cup chopped onion	
½ teaspoon minced garlic	1¼ teaspoons Italian seasoning, crushed
2 ¾ cups peeled and chopped tomatoes	
	¼ teaspoon white pepper

2 tablespoons dry white wine

1. Rinse, pat dry and quarter mushrooms (makes about 4 cups); set aside.
2. Heat oil in a large saucepan until hot.
3. Add onion and garlic; sauté until tender, about 3 minutes.
4. Add tomatoes, zucchini, green peppers, Italian seasoning, pepper and reserved mushrooms; simmer, covered, until vegetables are tender, about 15 minutes.
5. Stir in wine; continue to simmer, covered, 2 minutes.

Summertime Spaghetti with Vegetables & Cheese Sauce

Serves 4 to 6

2 tablespoons corn oil
1 zucchini, sliced
1 cup broccoli flowerets
2 cups sliced fresh mushrooms
1 cup peas
1 teaspoon salt

½ teaspoon Italian seasoning
¼ teaspoon instant minced
garlic
1 package (8 ounces) thin
spaghetti
Cheese Sauce

grated Parmesan or Romano cheese (optional)

1. Heat oil in a large skillet.
2. Add zucchini, broccoli, mushrooms, peas, salt, Italian seasoning and minced garlic; stir constantly, until tender-crisp.
3. Cover and keep warm.
4. Cook pasta according to package directions.
5. Combine Cheese Sauce and vegetables; heat through.
6. Serve over spaghetti with grated Parmesan or Romano cheese, if desired.

Cheese Sauce

2 tablespoons butter or
margarine
2 tablespoons flour

1½ cups milk
1 chicken-flavored bouillon cube
½ cup diced American cheese

1. Melt butter; blend in flour.
2. Gradually add milk and bouillon cube; stir and bring to a boil.
3. Remove from heat; add cheese, stirring until melted.

Mixed Garden Vegetable Bake

Serves 8

6 ears fresh corn
6 small zucchini, sliced
  ¼-inch thick
4 medium tomatoes, quartered
1 green pepper, thinly
  sliced
1 Bermuda onion, sliced and
  separated into rings

¼ cup butter, melted
1 tablespoon flour
1 teaspoon salt
1 teaspoon sugar
white pepper to taste
1 teaspoon chili powder
1 to 2 tablespoons grated
  Parmesan cheese

1. Cut corn off cobs with a sharp knife; use back of knife to scrape cobs.
2. Combine corn and other vegetables.
3. Heat butter in a small pan; stir in flour until smooth.
4. Add salt, sugar, pepper and chili powder.
5. Mix thoroughly with vegetables; pour into a greased 2-quart casserole.
6. Dust Parmesan cheese on top.
7. Bake in preheated 325° F. oven 1½ hours.

NOTE: Casserole can be prepared ahead of time and refrigerated.

Watercress & Endive Salad

Serves 4

2 heads Belgian endive
1 bunch fresh watercress
½ cup crumbled feta cheese
¼ cup chopped pecans

3 tablespoons vegetable oil
1 tablespoon freshly squeezed
   lemon juice
¼ teaspoon salt

⅛ teaspoon pepper

1. Cut endive into 2-inch pieces.
2. Tear watercress into bite-size pieces.
3. Arrange endive and watercress on salad plates; top with cheese and pecans.
4. Combine oil, lemon juice, salt and pepper; serve over salad.

Saucy Orange Yams

Serves 12

3 cans (17 ounces each) yams,
   well drained
1 can (6 ounces) frozen
   orange juice concentrate,
   thawed

½ cup light corn syrup
¼ cup firmly packed brown
   sugar
2 tablespoons margarine
orange slices (optional garnish)

1. Arrange yams in a single layer in a 13 × 9 × 2-inch greased baking dish; set aside.
2. Cook orange juice concentrate, corn syrup, brown sugar and margarine in a large skillet over medium heat until boiling; boil 10 minutes, or until thick and syrupy.
3. Pour sauce over yams.
4. Bake in preheated 325° F. oven, basting frequently, 20 to 25 minutes, or until heated.
5. Spoon into serving dish.
6. If desired, garnish with orange slices.

Carolina Yam Bread

Makes 1 loaf

1½ cups all-purpose flour
1½ teaspoons baking soda
½ teaspoon salt
¼ teaspoon ground cinnamon
¾ cup sugar
2 eggs, lightly beaten

½ cup vegetable oil
1 teaspoon pure vanilla
   extract
1½ cups grated North
   Carolina yams
1 cup chopped pecans

1. Combine flour, baking soda, salt and cinnamon in a large bowl.
2. Combine sugar, eggs, oil and vanilla in a small bowl; mix well.
3. Add egg mixture to dry ingredients; stir only until ingredients are blended.
4. Stir in yams and nuts.
5. Pour into a well-greased and floured 9 × 5-inch loaf pan.
6. Bake in preheated 350° F. oven 1 hour.
7. Cool 10 minutes; remove from pan and cool completely on wire rack.

North Carolina Home-Fried Yams

Serves 4

4 medium-size North Carolina
  yams (about 2¼ pounds)
3 tablespoons butter or
  margarine

3 tablespoons chopped onion
3 tablespoons chopped parsley
¼ teaspoon salt
dash of pepper

1. Wash and dry yams; prick with a fork.
2. Bake yams in preheated 400° F. oven 45 to 55 minutes until soft.
3. Cool yams to room temperature; chill thoroughly.
4. Peel and slice yams crosswise approximately ¼-inch thick; cut each slice into quarters.
5. Melt butter in a large skillet over medium heat; sauté yams 5 minutes, or until lightly brown. (Do not stir.)
6. Turn yams and cook 3 minutes longer.
7. Add onion, parsley, salt and pepper; cook, stirring occasionally, 2 to 3 minutes until onion is tender.

Scalloped Zucchini Squash with White Sauce

Serves 6

6 cups thinly sliced zucchini
  squash
1 cup boiling water
¾ cup Medium White Sauce
2 eggs, beaten
1 teaspoon salt

½ teaspoon original
  Worcestershire sauce
1 teaspoon minced onion
¼ cup fine dry bread crumbs
1 tablespoon butter or
  margarine, melted

1. Cook squash in boiling water until tender, about 5 minutes; drain.
2. Stir a little Medium White Sauce into beaten eggs; then gradually stir eggs into remaining sauce.
3. Stir in salt, Worcestershire sauce, onion and cooked squash.
4. Put in greased 1-quart casserole.
5. Mix bread crumbs with butter; sprinkle over squash mixture.
6. Bake in preheated 325° F. oven 35 minutes.

Medium White Sauce

1 tablespoon butter
2 tablespoons flour

¼ teaspoon salt
1 cup milk

1. Melt butter in a heavy saucepan; blend in flour until smooth.
2. Add salt.
3. Add milk slowly, stirring rapidly to prevent lumping.
4. Bring mixture to a boil, stirring constantly; reduce heat and cook 1 minute, stirring constantly.
5. Remove from heat.

Zucchini Bake

Serves 4 to 6

¼ cup light corn syrup
2 tablespoons corn oil

2 cloves garlic, minced
dash of salt

1 pound zucchini, sliced

1. Stir corn syrup, corn oil, garlic and salt in a 11 × 7 × 2-inch baking dish.
2. Add zucchini; toss to coat well.
3. Bake in preheated 375° F. oven, stirring occasionally, 35 minutes, or until fork-tender.

Zucchini Crunch

Serves 4

1 pound zucchini, sliced
1 tablespoon original
  Worcestershire sauce

4 tablespoons butter or
  margarine
pine nuts

1. Combine zucchini, Worcestershire sauce and butter in a saucepan; cook, covered, 12 minutes.
2. Remove to platter; sprinkle with toasted pine nuts.

Zucchini-Tomato Shashlik

Serves 4

1 medium green zucchini,
  cut into chunks
1 medium golden zucchini
  or other yellow summer
  squash, cut into chunks
8 cocktail tomatoes

1 green pepper, cut into
  small squares
4 medium onions, quartered
1 cup bottled Italian
  dressing

1. Marinate all vegetables in dressing at least 1 hour.
2. Arrange vegetables on skewers; grill over charcoal 20 minutes, or until tender.

NOTE: Great with barbecued steaks or fish!

Fresh Herbed Zucchini

Serves 6

2 pounds zucchini
2 tablespoons olive oil

1 teaspoon seasoned salt
½ teaspoon seasoned pepper

½ cup snipped fresh mint

1. Cut zucchini in half crosswise; cut into eighths lengthwise to form long sticks.
2. Heat oil in a large skillet; saute zucchini in oil over medium heat, stirring frequently, 10 minutes.
3. Sprinkle with seasoned salt, seasoned pepper and mint; cook 10 minutes longer, or until crisp-tender.

Zucchini Squash Sauté

Serves 6

3 tablespoons corn oil
¾ pound zucchini squash, diced
¾ pound yellow squash, diced
½ cup chopped onion
1 tablespoon salt

1 clove garlic, crushed
1 cup diced tomatoes
1 tablespoon original Worcestershire sauce
1 tablespoon tomato paste

1. Heat oil in a large skillet.
2. Add zucchini and yellow squash, onion and garlic; sauté 3 minutes, stirring carefully.
3. Combine and add remaining ingredients; simmer, covered, until vegetables are crisp-tender, about 8 to 10 minutes, stirring occasionally.

Cheddar Zucchini Supreme

Serves 6

2 tablespoons butter or margarine
6 cups thinly sliced fresh zucchini
1 teaspoon salt

⅛ teaspoon pepper
dash of garlic salt
1 can (8 ounces) tomato sauce
1 cup shredded Cheddar cheese, divided

1. Melt butter in a medium-size skillet.
2. Add zucchini, salt, pepper, garlic salt and tomato sauce; heat 10 minutes, stirring occasionally.
3. Add ½ cup cheese; stir until cheese is melted.
4. Pour into greased 1½-quart casserole; sprinkle with remaining cheese.
5. Bake in preheated 375° F. oven 20 minutes.

Cheese-Garlic Butter with Variations

Makes ½ cup

½ cup softened butter or margarine
¼ teaspoon garlic powder or few drops pressed garlic

¼ cup grated Parmesan cheese
dash of paprika (optional)

Combine all ingredients; spoon over vegetables.

Chili-Olive Butter (Variation)

Stir together ½ cup softened butter or margarine, ¼ teaspoon chili powder and 2 tablespoons minced pitted ripe olives.

Chive Butter (Variation)

Stir together ½ cup softened butter, 1 tablespoon minced chives and 2 teaspoons original Worcestershire sauce.

Herb Butter (Variation)

Stir together ½ cup softened butter, 1 teaspoon fresh lemon or lime juice, ½ teaspoon prepared mustard, ½ teaspoon basil leaves and ⅛ teaspoon original Worcestershire sauce. Add a dash of garlic powder, mixing well.

Dill Butter (Variation)

Stir together ½ cup softened butter, 2 teaspoons dill weed and 1 teaspoon onion salt.

Piquant Sauce

Makes 2 cups

1 package (8 ounces) cream cheese
½ teaspoon salt
⅛ teaspoon white pepper

¼ teaspoon dry mustard
⅛ teaspoon cayenne
2 eggs
2 tablespoons lemon juice

½ cup dairy sour cream

1. Cream the cream cheese at room temperature.
2. Add salt, pepper, mustard and cayenne.
3. Beat in eggs, one at a time; add lemon juice and sour cream, mixing well.
4. Heat thoroughly in double boiler over simmering but not boiling water, stirring often.
5. Serve over asparagus, green beans, broccoli or artichokes.

Dill Sauce

Makes 1½ cups

2 tablespoons butter
1 tablespoon flour
⅛ teaspoon white pepper

1 teaspoon chicken broth
½ cup water
1 cup dairy sour cream

1 tablespoon dill weed

1. Melt butter.
2. Add flour, white pepper, broth and water; cook over low heat, stirring, until mixture thickens.
3. Remove from heat.
4. Stir in sour cream and dill; heat but do not boil.
5. Serve over boiled potatoes, broccoli, green beans, cauliflower, peas, asparagus or carrots.

Polonaise Sauce for Vegetables

Makes about ½ cup

¼ cup butter
¼ cup fine bread crumbs

1 tablespoon lemon juice
pinch of salt

1. Melt butter in a small saucepan.
2. Add bread crumbs, lemon juice and salt; heat until golden brown.
3. Pour over vegetables.
4. Especially good on broccoli, green beans, cauliflower, brussels sprouts and carrots.

Asparagus Sauce

Serves 4 to 6

2 egg yolks
1 tablespoon tarragon
  vinegar or lemon juice
1 cup dairy sour cream

½ teaspoon salt
½ teaspoon paprika
1 teaspoon Angostura
  aromatic bitters

1. Place egg yolks, tarragon vinegar and sour cream in top of a small double boiler; stir over gently boiling water until sauce begins to thicken.
2. Beat in salt, paprika and Angostura aromatic bitters.
3. Place asparagus on heated platter and pour sauce over the stalks. ter and pour

Cucumber Sauce

Makes 1 pint

1 cup finely chopped, peeled
  cucumbers
½ cup heavy cream
2 tablespoons cider vinegar

¼ teaspoon salt
¹⁄₁₆ teaspoon ground white
  pepper
½ teaspoon paprika

1. Drain cucumbers well; set aside.
2. Beat cream until thick but not stiff.
3. Gradually beat in vinegar; beat until cream stands in soft peaks.
4. Fold in drained cucumbers, salt, white pepper and paprika.
5. Serve over molded fish or egg salads.

Mustard Sauce for Broccoli, Microwaved

Makes about 1 cup

1 can (10½ ounces) chicken
  gravy

¼ cup pimiento strips
2 teaspoons prepared mustard

1. Combine all ingredients in a 2-cup glass measure; cover with plastic wrap.
2. Microwave on HIGH 3 to 4 minutes, or until hot.
3. Let stand, covered, 2 minutes.
4. Serve over cooked asparagus or broccoli.

NOTE: Deliciously simple and a great way to dress up a green vegetable!

IGM-1W/9-E8000-6/1608